Ever since Olga Korbut captured the imagination of the world with her astounding 1972 Olympic performance, gymnastic competitions have been media events. And gymnasts, such as Nadia Comaneci, Maria Filatova, Cathy Rigby and Nelli Kim have become international stars. They are idolized by youngsters around the world!

Gymnastics is truly a sport whose time has come!

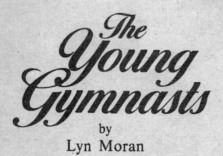

The Young Gymnasts

by
Lyn Moran

A Giniger Book

tempo
books

GROSSET & DUNLAP
A FILMWAYS COMPANY
Publishers • New York

Cover photos:
Front: Pictured is Silvia Hindorff of the German Democratic Republic. *Photo by Alan E. Burrows*

Back: Maria Filatova or "Masha," as she is affectionately called, of the Soviet Union. *Photo by Alan E. Burrows*

THE YOUNG GYMNASTS
Copyright © 1978 by The K.S. Giniger Company, Inc.
Published simultaneously in Canada

ISBN: 0-448-17019-1

A Tempo Books Original
Published by arrangement with The K.S. Giniger Company, Inc., 235 Park Avenue South, New York, New York 10003

Printed in the United States of America

ACKNOWLEDGMENTS

The author acknowledges her debt of gratitude to the gymnastics federations of Canada, the Federal Republic of Germany, The Netherlands, Poland, Romania, Spain, Sweden and Switzerland, to the Embassy of the USSR, and to the Novosti Press Agency for their helpfulness; and wishes to thank the fine photographers from all over the world who responded so promptly to her requests for photographs.

CONTENTS

Heike Kunhardt *(Alan E. Burrows)*

Chapter 1

Introduction:
The World of Gymnastics

Because some countries now have thousands of young gymnasts, it is too hard to write about them all. In this book, I have taken a few of the better young gymnasts in each country and will tell you about them. Each of them is special, or unlike any other, and the best word to describe them is unique. Olga and Nadia and Maria and Nelli—they are unique. And, because they are, other youngsters want to be like them. They look at the way Nadia or Olga do a gymnastic trick (a type of move) and try to do the same. In the last Olympics, the most exciting gymnast was a tiny girl, Maria Filatova. Maria, or Masha as she is also known, is from the Soviet Union and many other aspiring younger gymnasts watched in awe as she, tiny as she was, completed many difficult routines.

All over the world, there are beginners in gymnastics. No two are alike. Of these, a few will become champions because they are able to work harder, or able to train longer, or have better coaching. Some will stay in gymnastics because they like to work on the balance beam, or bars. But others will want to compete and to win.

Whether you want just to take part because it's fun, or whether you want to go out there in front of a lot of people who will judge you, will be up to you. You can even sit in the stands and just watch this exciting sport. Then you and your friends can judge and say what you think the score should be. If you are not good enough to beat the others, it doesn't matter. There are so many things you can do in this sport to work with others. You might even be able to say that you helped someone else win a medal.

This is a great time to be in this sport of gymnastics. You could be another big star, or a coach, or a judge, or sit in the stands and watch. You will always learn, and always have fun, just as little Masha has fun or as Olga used to. It can be a new and exciting time for you.

Chapter 2

Stars of the Seventies

Since 1970, the gymnasts who have become world stars are Olga Korbut, Ludmilla Tourischeva, Nadia Comaneci and Maria Filatova. There have been others, of course, like Cathy Rigby of the United States, Teodora Ungureanu from Romania, and the USSR's Nelli Kim. The first four became the idols of young girls all over the world—Nadia and Maria because of the 1976 Olympics in Montreal, and Olga and Ludmilla because of the years before.

Ludmilla was the first girl to be known all over the world for gymnastics. She did not have the pert face of Olga Korbut, but she was lovely and full of grace. She was a member of the winning Soviet team in Mexico in 1968, but was so young that she did not do well. In 1969, she was the third all around in the European Championships and, by 1970, she had become the very best in the world. In Yugoslavia, where the World Championships were held, all the people crowded around Ludmilla, the new world champion. She became European champion again in the Soviet Union in 1971 and all the Russians were thrilled about this.

In 1972, the Olympics were held at Munich in the Federal Republic of Germany (West Germa-

Ludmilla Tourischeva   *(Courtesy International Gymnast)*

ny). We all know who had the most impact here! Olga, of course. Although Ludmilla actually won again, with many gold medals, it was Olga, the little ponytailed girl, who had the most impact there. Ludmilla was the all around champion once more in the European Championships in 1973 and the World Champion titleholder yet again in 1974. She won the World Cup in England in 1975. Then, at the European Championships in Norway, a new face was seen. Nadia Comaneci, whose name people learned to pronounce *Nahdeeah Komaneesh,* was a skinny little girl who took the crowd by surprise. They did not expect her to do well because Ludmilla was to be the best. Instead, Ludmilla came behind Nadia, who was very much younger, being only 13 then. This was the start of Nadia and the end for Ludmilla, who never again won a major competition. But Ludmilla did continue to win gold medals, as always, in single events. At Montreal, she won medals for being second in vault and floor exercise, third in the all around and best gymnast on the Soviet team.

Because Nadia was very thin and not well built like Ludmilla, people saw her as a little child. Until Nadia, the only other gymnast to have become famous while being child-like, was Olga Korbut. Olga was never a "perfect" gymnast. She didn't get a lot of 10.00 scores, which is the best score one can get under the rules of the F.I.G. (International Gymnastic Federation). The F.I.G. gives a gymnast a high score of 10.00 if there are no mistakes, errors or breaks in the movements at all. Perfect scores were a very rare thing indeed until Nadia. Nelli Kim has also had a ten, Teodora Ungureanu has had a ten in Romania and, in the United States, Kelly McCoy, Marcia Frederick and Muriel Grossfeld have received tens in American competition.

Olga was a very exciting gymnast. She was bright, happy and loved the crowds and liked to perform in front of people. At 4 feet 11 inches, Olga was small, but she was full of life, and her floor exercise made the crowd roar for more! Her childish wiggles and dance moves were just right for Olga. She waved at people as she danced around, always with a big smile. The press loved her also. Unafraid to show her emotions, Olga laughed and cried and sometimes even yelled. Reporters found her to be an exciting personality because she said and did things which they found

Olga Korbut   *(Alan E. Burrows)*

were interesting to write about.

In Munich, Olga won gold medals for her balance beam and floor exercise and a silver medal for her routine on the uneven bars. She was very happy about this and said so. Ludmilla won the all around. And Nadia, who was then too young, didn't yet capture the attention of gymnastic enthusiasts.

When Olga was on tour with her team, each time they went to another country people lined up for hours to see her, although many knew nothing about gymnastics.

In the all around placings in the 1976 Olympics, Olga finished in fifth place. She was limping, because of an injury. Nothing stopped her, however. She wouldn't let her fans down. Although she was tired and hurt, she kept smiling and doing her best. Her uneven bar routine brought her a great score, 9.90, and she also got a 9.90 for her beam in the finals. No one will ever forget how Olga, that outspoken, daring, and always exciting Russian girl, had changed gymnastics.

The slender, sad-looking Romanian started a new group of fans. With her pale skin and huge eyes, her droopy mouth and her youth, she looked just like a china doll. Men and women, boys and girls, all liked Nadia. People wanted her to win, because she seemed so very sad. Those long slim legs and the body without hips made Nadia seem just like a child. That is what they called her. "The child Nadia."

When she was born on November 12, 1961, Gheorghe and Stefania Comaneci looked at the little baby and were happy. Nadia was the name chosen for this star of the future. The town she was born in has two names, Onesti and Gheorghe

Nadia Comaneci   *(Tom Salvas)*

Nadia Comaneci   *(© 1977 Linsey Scott Barrington)*

Gheorghiu Dej. One is the old name and, as happens in some countries, the name was changed to honor a hero. But the people still call it Onesti. And all over the world it is now known as the home of Nadia Comaneci, youthful star of the gymnastics world.

When she was seven, she took part in a gymnastics meet. When she was eight, Nadia entered the Romanian National Competition for Juniors. She ended up in thirteenth place. At this time she had as her coach a man called Bela Karolyi, who was to one day make her world famous. Bela was very kind to Nadia and treated her just like his own daughter. When she won the all around title in a Romania-Poland meet the year after winning the junior national title in 1970, people started to talk about her. Nadia was known in Europe as Comaneci, just as Olga was called Korbut. In East European countries, people often use the second name first; this is known as the "family" name. The Chinese do the same thing. Ludmilla was always called Tourischeva and the great Czech gymnast, Vera Caslavska, always only Caslavska.

Nadia began winning medals and gaining recognition. People were pointing and cheering, during her routines, but they did not feel about her they way they did about Olga. Many people thought Nadia was too serious. She jumped onto the beam and did her routine and then she was off, and over to her coach. If she saw the crowd, she did not show it. But she was very, very good and her scores, for her age, were very high. Bela Karolyi was excited about this. He knew she was someone very special.

It was in Norway at the European Championships that Nadia first became known outside her own country. She did not do simple tricks, but the hard ones. Her Tsukahara, that most difficult vault with its one and a half backward somersault from a cartwheel, brought Nadia a score of 9.80. Her uneven bar routine was even higher at 9.90. Because she could get no higher than 10.00 her scores were great for a young new gymnast. And so it was that better-known, older gymnasts were beaten by a little girl called Nadia.

Karolyi was thrilled! Nadia's parents were excited and, although she did not show it, their daughter was excited too. She had tried very hard and had been unsure of herself but now she had won and knew what she could do. The Romanian gymnastic chiefs thought it was time to enter Nadia in another big meet. At only 13 years old Nadia went to Canada, where they were to have the Pre-Olympics, which was the year before the 1976 Olympic Games. Her routines and tricks were almost perfect, and the crowd cheered and cheered this skinny, sad-looking child. When she won the all around title with ease, Karolyi knew that she was ready for the Olympics.

Americans did not yet know that much about Nadia—not until she trotted out onto the mat at Madison Square Garden in New York. This was for the event known as the American Cup. And, again, Nadia was ready. She raised her hand to the judges, but showed nothing on her face. A few weeks earlier she had been in a meet in Arizona where she had been given 9.90 scores. The gymnastic fans knew Nadia. They had been watching her. Most people outside of the sport did not, and they were very amazed at what they saw. For, here in New York, Nadia was given two perfect scores of ten! The crowd went wild! Everyone cheered the little Romanian girl. Her coach grinned with pride. He and his wife, Marta, knew this day would come. This was, after all, not the first perfect score for Nadia. She had had one back in 1975 in the Romanian Nationals and also in a competition in Kitchener, Canada, the same year.

England saw Nadia in 1976 and the British fans were thrilled! "Bravo, Nadia," they yelled. Small boys and girls lined up to get a look at her as she walked by. In Nadia, they could see themselves. She also was still a child, a teenager. The British gymnastic people said they had never seen anyone like her. Everyone talked about the coming Olympics and how she would do against Olga. Olga had not been doing too well, and had been injured again and again. Her fans were to be found all over the world still, and they stuck by her. Nadia's fans were not the same. They were fans because of her perfect scores, and not because of her sunny smile and ability to get along with the fans, as was the case with Olga.

Where Olga Korbut made mistakes, Nadia did not. Her routines were done with skill and almost without fault. Judges were happy to watch Nadia, because she was so good, and they all agreed on the high scores given her. Nadia was so used to doing well at age 14, she took all the praise without saying anything. This made a lot of people unhappy. They said she was too calm, that she should show some feelings. Then they said she was like a robot, doing all her tricks so well, but her face showing no smile or happiness. Olga also had upset people, but this was because Olga said things about others who were not as good as she was. Olga also was seen as a big star and the gymnasts in her country did not like her to be other than a team member.

People pointed to Ludmilla. Ludmilla, they said, had always smiled and had been kind to everyone. She had been loved by little children and old ladies. She would never have upset anyone, no matter how cruel they were to her. And they were right when they said that neither Olga nor Nadia were anything like Ludmilla. All three were very unlike each other.

In Montreal, people paid a lot of money to get tickets to the Forum, where Nadia, Olga and the pretty Nelli Kim were to appear. Would Olga beat Nadia? Would Ludmilla beat Nelli? Would Nadia beat Nelli, as she had done before? The crowds at each performance were excited. Some called for Nadia, some for Olga. Olga, they said, was nursing a sore foot, and looked very tired and in pain. Nadia was, well, just Nadia! A little more cheerful than she had been, but no teasing of teammates like Olga. And, for the three well-known girls, there was something else to worry about—a very, *very* small gymnast from Siberia. She could not see over the horse, she was so small. Her hair was in ponytails and her eyes shone with fun. She giggled a lot and laughed at the coaches. She ran to help them when they moved things, although she weighed so little. The people who came to watch Nadia and Olga found their eyes going more and more to this tiny girl with the sunny smile. Her name was Maria Filatova, known also as Masha.

When the Olympics were over, Nadia Comaneci of Romania, a slight figure in white who had just made history, was the new champion. There had been no battle between Olga and Nadia, although Nelli Kim had made a game attempt and had been given a perfect ten. Nadia had won the all around title, the uneven bars, and the beam titles. Nelli Kim beat Nadia in the floor exercise and in vaulting. It was in vault that Nadia did the worst and in which Nelli almost got another ten, with a score of 9.95. Olga did well, despite her injury. She, too, got scores like 9.90, and how her fans loved this! Despite the pain, she kept on trying.

Nelli Kim *(© Alan E. Burrows)*

When it was all over, the radio, television and newspapers told the world about little Nadia. Nadia's parents swelled with pride. Thousands of Romanians boasted about their great national heroine. Hundreds swarmed into the airport to greet her coming home. Nadia! Nadia! And now Nadia smiled, and was seen laughing as she hugged yet another of the many dolls she collects. She had dolls from all over the world now, while she herself was still doll-sized. And now she had won a lot more tens! Olga's fans did not leave her. They did not care that she had not won more medals. She had waved at them and smiled, and each time she did a trick they knew she was doing it just for them.

The lovely, mature Ludmilla Tourischeva comforted Olga, as she had done often in the past. Ludmilla did not win any title other than the one she shared with Nelli, of being the best on the Soviet team. Ludmilla knew now that she must retire, and she told the people of the press that she would do so that year. She said she wanted to become a coach and to pass on to others all the things she had learned as a gymnast.

The tiniest competitor, that pixie with the impish face, did in fact cause more comment than Olga, Nadia or Ludmilla together. The fans in the stands loved her and yelled for more! Little Maria Filatova gave them what they wanted. Only 4 foot 6 ½ inches tall, she did look a lot like someone they all remembered back in 1972. Oh, not in her face or hair, but in her ways. She reminded people of Olga —Olga's impishness and her grin; Olga's pert charm and her love of people. This, too, was Maria, and Maria was also a very good gymnast. Her scores for someone barely fifteen were worth telling about. In the events prior to the finals,

Maria Filatova   *(© Volker Hischen)*

Maria had in her combined scores made 77.05.
This made her ninth along with two others. She
had been given in these events scores of 9.75, 9.85
and 9.90. Not bad for someone shorter than the
horse! It was too bad that, under the rules, Maria
could not go into the finals. Only three girls from
each country could do that, and the ones from the
USSR who made it were Olga, Nelli and Ludmilla.

Maria may have been small, but she was a tough
little girl from Siberia and she was going to show
the world what someone of her size could do. Now
that the Olympics were over, Maria would work
toward the Grand Prix in Paris and the well-known
Moscow News meet in her native land. Siberia is
just one of the many republics in the great Soviet
Union.

In Paris, Filatova caught the eye again when she
won the all around title. True, not many famous
gymnasts took part so it was not a fair test. Her
coach was well satisfied. It had been when Masha
was even tinier and very young that a man called
Innokenti Mametjev first saw her and wondered
how someone so very small could be so full of life.
It just might be that he could make a gymnast out
of her! So it was that Filatova took those first steps
into the sports school where she was to learn so
much. She had a mind of her own and used it. She
often told her coach, who is well known as a trainer
in Europe, what she wanted to do—and she was
often right. Sometimes she tried things which were
too hard for her tiny frame. So Mametjev gave her
tricks to do which were just right. Maria wanted to
do well and she wanted to prove herself.

It had been in 1975 in Japan that gymnastic fans
had really seen the little Siberian. She finished in

fifth place in the very popular Chunichi Cup. People talked about her doing a double back somersault, a really rare thing for gymnasts. They did not know Masha. Small she was, but she had great courage. She would try any trick, any move.

In 1977, Filatova went into the *Moscow News* meet. When it was over, she had won the all around title and later, in Riga, she again won the all around title, although well-known gymnasts from dozens of countries entered. Maria blew kisses to the fans, waved at anyone who waved at her and helped everyone move the equipment. She really loved to be in competitions and she loved the people who watched her!

She did not win the European Championships, but she did win a silver medal in floor exercise and a bronze for beam. The future was bright for Maria and she made the most of it. She went on a very unusual tour in the summer of 1977. She and dozens of other gymnasts from all over the world went to Brazil to give displays at many cities. The biggest hit was little Filatova! She chatted in German, French or Russian to people who spoke English and somehow they were able to understand her. She always tried, even if she had to write words or make signs. This was the way Filatova was. She was able to be a bridge between people from other lands. She looked like a child, yet she was very wise and sensible. And by now she was 4 feet 7½ inches and her face was quite pretty, with happy eyes and rosebud mouth.

While Maria competed she kept making more and more friends. When her team toured England, people forgot about Olga being there, or that Nelli went home sick. Maria was just as exciting. In the 1978 *Moscow News* meet Maria was second all around, winning gold medals for her balance beam and uneven bars. At the Soviet championships, Filatova was beaten out by Elena Muckhina for first place. When Maria won those medals, someone standing on the sidelines was seen to cry with happiness. That person was none other than Maria's coach, the great Ludmilla Tourischeva! Yes, Ludmilla was now a coach and devoted to younger girls, who loved her dearly. Although Elena Muckhina beat Maria for the gold medal in the 1978 Soviet championships, Filatova's coaches were quite pleased with her silver medal. That she had come so far, although smaller than anyone else in competition, was a great credit to her.

Olga meanwhile had gone on to marriage. The gay, smiling gymnast of the 1972 Olympics married a tall, pleasant young man called Leonid Bortkevich, a singer with a popular music group. They went to Cuba for their honeymoon and later Olga said she too would become a coach. Olga is heavier now and wears make-up and earrings but still has the bright, toothy smile which made her world famous. She will never lose that.

Ludmilla added beauty to the sport, but Olga gave it life. She was always so full of humor and wit people could not help but like her. Korbut was a name known even in small countries by people who were not fans of gymnastics. She brought many more gymnasts—boys and girls—into the sport. Until 1972, gymnastics was not a big sport at all and then along came Olga. Olga was the one who made it a talked-about sport throughout the whole world. Newspapers wrote about her and gymnastics. Some had big stories on the front page. Olga was even taken to meet the President of the United States. Everywhere people of all ages knew that she was a gymnast, and gymnasts today say that she made their sport famous.

Nadia was beginning to have trouble in 1977. The worst thing was what took place at the European Championships which were held in Prague, Czechoslovakia. All the famous gymnasts were there. It was very exciting because Nelli Kim was the chief rival of Comaneci and people did not know which would win. Nelli has always been one of the best vaulters in the world and Nadia is not. Nadia has been much better on beam, floor and bars. Anyway, in Prague, both girls had to face other great stars and this made it hard.

Before the meet started, the judges said that they would give more credit to the more difficult vaults. This means they would give a higher score if the vault was a harder one than others. Nelli Kim did her vault, a very hard one, called a full twisting Tsukahara. Her second vault was a straight Tsukahara—another hard one. She was given scores of 9.75 and 9.70 for these two vaults. When Nadia's turn came, she, too, did well. She did a piked Tsukahara and a tucked Tsukahara (you can find out about these in the chapter about gymnastic terms in this book). Nadia also got a 9.75 score and a 9.70. The crowd buzzed with excitement! What would happen now? Even little Maria Filatova got a 9.70 for her Tsukahara vault, but her first vault was lower.

What officials do is to add the scores together and then divide them into two equal parts. If the scores are 10.00 and 10.00, they add up to 20. So they say that half of 20 is 10.00 and the "average" is also 10.00. If you have 9.25 and 9.75 and add these two, you get 19. Half of 19 is 9.50. The average shown on the scoreboard then would be 9.50.

This means you could have a poor vault *and* a very good one. It would not matter about the poor one because, when they add the scores of both of them and then cut it in half to get a fair score, it could still be the winner.

Well, the people from the Soviet Federation were upset and the people from the Romanian Federation were upset. Both wanted their gymnast's scores to be raised. The Russians said Nelli Kim's vault was harder. The Romanians thought Nadia's was. The Russians won. Nelli's score was brought up by a little bit to 9.775. This was added to the score she had from the first day's competition and gave her a total of 19.525. Nadia's score was also raised to 9.750 and this was added to her first day's score, for a total of 19.500. This made Kim the winner of the vault title.

The Romanians had wanted Nadia to win, of course. But Nelli's vault was very, very good. The Romanian girls did not worry. They were there to do their best and they had already won medals. By this time, Nadia had won the all around title and had tied with Muckhina in the bars event in this last session. The balance beam was next and all the girls did their routines. Muckhina and Nadia were the best. Nadia's was a very fine exercise and she was happy with it. Then came Teodora. She was into her routine when someone called out. They were told to stop at once. The crowd gasped. What was happening? Before they had time even to think, they saw the whole team of Romanian girls walk out of the arena with their coaches! People were shocked. Such a thing had never happened before. This was indeed an exciting meet!

Later, everyone was told why. The Romanian Gymnastic Federation had been in touch with the

Karolyis after they had seen the change in the vault scores. They were very annoyed by this. They thought it was wrong and they were going to protest. They said that the team must all go home at once. Bela and Marta and the girls had to leave for the hotel and then the airport. It was very sad for them because Nadia could have won more medals. As it was, they had to forfeit the medals in the events in which they had taken part in the finals because they did not finish the competition. Teodora had not even completed her beam routine when the walkout took place.

In the news later that year, there was talk of Nadia having problems in her club. Nadia was not getting along with Karolyi, people said, but everyone laughed at that. Nadia, meanwhile, was still collecting dolls and now had a huge number. She also had started to collect postal stamps. This was mainly because so many people wrote her from all over the world and she was able to do it with ease. She was doing well in school with her French and English. By now, she could speak English and, by 1978, would be in the tenth grade.

All this time Nadia still had her best friend. Teodora Ungureanu had known Nadia since both girls were very small. The two were very close. Year after year, they had gone to each other's homes, shared each other's dolls. Then came a time when Nadia needed her friend. But Teodora became ill and was kept out of the meets. That was in 1977. Nadia was upset and she worried about her friend.

Again, in 1978, the newspapers said Nadia was not pleased with Karolyi. People said that he was no longer paying Nadia enough attention and she was not doing well. They said Karolyi had other hobbies and his gymnasts no longer took up his whole time. It was not long before the news came that Nadia had been sent to Dynamo Bucaresti, a very well-known Bucharest club in which other top Romanian girls also performed. Her new coach was named Bela Kovacs. For some months all was quiet, and no one knew what Nadia was doing.

The summer came, and the Romanian team appeared in Italy. Nadia was expected to get high scores, and it was said that the judges did make them higher than they should. Even so, she was in great form with several more tens. If the scoring was high, the 9.90 which might have been more fair, was still a very fine score for any world gymnast. It looked as though she would be able to compete once again at her top level.

People felt let down when Nadia performed in a French display, however. She had many fumbles on her beam and seemed unsteady in other events. Because she was not being scored, it did not matter. The nice thing was that Teodora was with her once again, and looked in good health. They gave a funny rock music display for the fans and Nadia was great! She rocked and laughed with the other young girls and it was just like old times, with Teodora smiling. The crowd cheered and Nadia waved at them. Now Nadia was happy again, and could think about her performance and how to cope with her 5 feet 3 inch frame and extra weight.

The team went to China, that great land with the world's largest population. In Shanghai, the Romanian girls were beaten by the Chinese, and one Chinese girl got a 9.95! Nadia was in great form. The people loved her, as they love all gymnasts. Her scoring was high, and she did her very best to please the crowd. This girl is the one who was in

Montreal and who won the Olympic title. Some people even said she now had more skills!

So, the little girl image of Nadia disappeared. She is taller and mature. The little girl image of Maria has vanished. She is still shorter than others, but now has the face and manner of an adult. Both girls have changed their hair style and both are pretty. They will continue to compete.

Can Ludmilla's gymnast Maria Filatova win the world titles that Ludmilla herself won in competition? Maybe; maybe not. For Nadia is still here.

But, at the October 1978 world championships in Strasbourg, France, Maria and other Russians consistently outpointed Nadia.

Olga and Ludmilla are still in the sport. Like Nelli, both are married women. They will not compete in the Olympics ahead, but their gymnasts probably will. These two great young women have given years to the sport. They have made girls and boys all the world over want to be gymnasts. They each gave special meaning to gymnastics. During the 1970s Ludmilla was first, then Olga, then Nadia and Maria.

In the United States, Cathy Rigby was the girl young Americans admired most. Cathy was all they wanted to be, because at that time American gymnasts had not won world titles. They wanted to be Cathys, but they hoped, too, someday to become Nadias. That day is now here. Young Americans have won gold medals abroad.

Olga, Nadia, Ludmilla—they led the way. They will always be known as the gymnasts who did the most to make the sport popular. More names will be added in the years ahead. But none will ever gain the love, awe and respect awarded to those "Big Three."

Chapter 3

The Soviet Union

Korbut, Kim, Tourischeva, Filatova, Grosdova
—what magic in those names! When we think of
gymnastics, we think Russian. When we hear these
names we can "see" the Russian or Soviet girls.
Years ago it was ballet and Russia. Now, it is gymnastics and the Russians.

We should know that the country is called the
Union of Soviet Socialist Republics and *not*
Russia. Russia is only one state within the USSR.
We need to know this so that we do not call a gymnast from Armenia a Russian. She would not like
that at all. She may speak the Russian language,
but she is from the Soviet Union. The young Soviet
gymnasts today are as good as ever. In fact, many
people say that they will be better than previous
Soviet gymnasts. There are more girls now becoming gymnasts, so they have more to chose from.
Remember, this is a huge country with 260 million
people. This means that they have lots more girls
who want to be gymnasts than years ago.

Let us have a look at how their system works. In
the Soviet Union, the state gives lessons to anyone
who wants to take them, in any sport. This means
that a young girl can go to school for reading, writ-
ing and math but also to be trained as a gymnast.

They also have gymnastics in factories and in industry. When they have what we call a coffee break, the people who work there are given time to do physical exercises or gymnastics.

If they had a beginner of around 7 years old, she would take gymnastics two hours a day three days a week, and if she were 8 and in the third junior grade it would be the same. Then, in the second junior grade, at 9, she would have one hour more a week; and, in the first junior grade, she would have lessons three to four times a week for three hours a day. After that, there is third advance grade, second advance grade, and first advance grade, ending with the best—the pre-elite and the elite. We also use the word elite and it means the pick or best of something.

If a young girl is afraid of falling, she need not worry; in the Soviet Union, they use pits filled with foam. She can fall from the bars and not get hurt. More and more countries are using these pits now, which is a very good thing. Ballet and dance is taught at all levels to gymnasts. This teaches the girls how to move well and how to be graceful.

Awards are given when one gets to a higher level. There is a Master of Sport award, which is the highest, which Olga Korbut and Ludmilla Tourischeva hold. For the years after 1978, the Soviet federation issued new ways to rank gymnasts. The junior grade comes first, with the lowest being grade 3. After that comes the junior rank or grade 2. Then comes rank or grade 1 junior. There are no more ranks for juniors, because the adult ranking comes next. It also is adult ranking 3, 2, and 1. Above that comes the Candidate to Master of Sport. The word "candidate" is one we hear often in politics. In this case, it means a gymnast who is seeking a certain goal or honor. This one would be the Master of Sport. The Master of Sport is the top Soviet ranking within their country but there is another called Master of Sport, International Class.

Although all these titles have to be earned by gymnasts by doing well in meets, titles such as Merited Master of Sport and Master of Sport, International Class, can be given to someone by the state for outstanding efforts or gains. When a gymnast gets enough scores, her name is sent to the Central Committe for Sports and the gymnast will then get a certificate and lapel pin.

Let us look at the system for scoring. In an all around meet a gymnast would have to have seventy-five or more points in the Soviet Championships or USSR Cup and be in the first six places. This would get the prized Master of Sport, International Class, award. In single (individual) events, the gymnast would have to be first, second or third. In the European Championships, she would have to be in the first three places in single events and the first six places in all around. In the Olympic Games, she would be required to end up in the first ten places in the all around and in the first six places in single events. For other meets, such as the *Moscow News,* Riga Tournament, World University Games, etc., she would have to finish in first place in the individuals, and in the first three places in the all around. In groups for the Candidate for Master of Sports, points have to be earned. It is 72, at least, in every case, even for the schoolchildren's Spartakiade. Everyone, boys and girls alike, gets graded for every championship or every competition in which they appear.

As you can see, this gives Soviet boys and girls always something to compete for at every level.

They get awards for everything they win from the age of 8 and up. The Soviet girls aim for this Master of Sports Award first. They know that only six or seven girls can make an Olympic team, so they try for something nearer their reach first. Anyone can try, of course, but not many ever make it. To them, the joy of taking part is worth it. They like to perform in local meets and in nationals. The Olympics is something that they all hope for, but there are other things also.

One thing the coaches at the sports school do is have gymnastic students watch each other perform and then they are asked to say what they think about the routine. They give what they think the score should be. It has been said that there is too much truth in what is heard and it sometimes makes the girls cry! But it is all good learning.

The sports schools are run by industry or trade unions and other groups. These schools train the girls after normal school hours in the three sport rankings. They are the base for all the new ideas. They prepare the young girls for what lies ahead. To see how well they do, we now take a look at some young Soviet gymnasts of today.

We know that Olga, Ludmilla, Nelli and the tiny Filatova have been the "big stars" during the past years. Elena Muckhina was very high on the Soviet list during 1977, but she proved to be a girl with ups and downs. She was good in one meet and poor in the next. The Soviet coaches were very puzzled. She had a very fine uneven bars routine, but it was not enough to carry her through a meet. Then, suddenly, they had several great young gymnasts! Svetlana Agapova, Natalia Shaposhnikova, Natasha Tereschenko, Tatiana Arshannikova— new magical names! By now, the Soviet Union needed someone to replace Olga and Ludmilla; Nelli Kim was out of action with an appendix operation.

It was hard to find someone good enough to fill such famous shoes. The choice was finally between two girls, Svetlana Agapova and Natalia Shaposhnikova, with another, Natasha Tereschenko, running third. Shaposhnikova was born in 1961 and is with the Dynamo Rostov Club of Rastorotsky. Rostov-on-Don is the home of the world-famous Ludmilla Tourischeva also. But Natalia did not look at all like Ludmilla. She has a wide flat face, with snub nose and wide slanting eyes. While she may not have looked like Ludmilla as far as her face went, she did everywhere else! She had the grace, the arm moves, the leg moves. She used her big, slanting eyes, just as Ludmilla did. It was not long before people were calling Shaposhnikova the "new Tourischeva." In the 1977 *Moscow News* meet, the little girl from Rostov risked the piked double somersault on her floor routine. This was very hard. Then she did something that the lovely, graceful Svetlana Grosdova does so well. She did a one-handed balance on the beam. But the routine which made her a big hit everywhere was her floor exercise to the delightful music from the opera *Carmen.* This is called "The Toreador's Song," and, as done by Natalia, was just great! The music refers to the men who go out to fight the big bulls in the arenas in Mexico and Spain. Well, to see her was to "see" the bull, and the crowd, and the capes whirling. The Russian girl swayed and danced, and leaped, and used her hands as horns. She looked just like a bull at that time! Then she did what the bullfighter does, and pretended to use the cape. It was a really fine routine and got her a good score.

Natalia Shaposhnikova   *(Norbert Smyk)*

Svetlana Agapova   *(Alan E. Burrows)*

From then on, Natalia was everyone's favorite.

But that same night there was another meet. This was what is known as an "unofficial" meet, where girls too young for the big meet are allowed to take part. In this competition, many new names showed up. Among these was a 12-year-old called Elena Naimushina. Elena did very well for her age, and people told themselves that this was a gymnast to watch. But there were so many others also! Sacharova, Sentschenko, Gontschenko, Glutschenko, Schidunova—was there no end to the talent in this vast land?

Galina Glutschenko was 14 years old in 1977. She is from the RSFSR Club in Rostov-on-Don. She trains with Mrs. Swojlova, not with the better-known coaches. She is also coached by Lyubov Miromanova, who was in charge of the Soviet team in a meet against the East Germans. In this meet, Galina got huge scores for her age—9.65 on bars and floor and 9.75 for bars in the finals. The people who saw her then said she performed like the famous Ludmilla.

When the team went to Poland later, they were part of a seventy-girl group from eleven countries. Galina ended in sixth place. Not bad! Again she had a fine score for her uneven bars, 9.70. She did well enough that the Soviet federation thought they should send her to Canada for the Ontario Cup in 1977. Glutschenko did not let them down. She came second all around in Toronto and third all around in Regina. From Canada, she went to Spain and the Barcelona Invitational. Here Galina beat all comers to win the title. Oddly enough, Glutschenko only came in eighth in the Junior Championships in Minsk in Russia, being beaten by Arshannikova as well as Gontschenko—both of whom she was able to beat earlier that same year.

Japan was where a delightful gymnast came to the fore. Her name was Svetlana Agapova. She is very slender, reddish blonde, with a rather short face. She is not what we would expect someone from the Soviet Union to look like. By that, I mean we look for the Nelli, Ludmilla, Natalia types—heavier and dark-eyed. Agapova is a tiny girl, with a catchy grin. She wears her hair in a ponytail. One thing she did in the Japanese meet was to make a one-armed catch to the low bar, a really unusual move. She has slim legs and very mobile hands, which she uses a lot in her routines. She is a dainty girl. She points her toes just right and her chin juts out as she does her lovely balance beam routine.

She is, of course, still very young, having been born in 1964. She, too, is with the well-known RSFSR club. Because of her age, she has not been entered in too many meets yet where she will face better gymnasts. In Vilnius, Russia, a large number of girls under the age of 14 went into a meet against each other. The girl who won was Ina Mitrofinova, the same gymnast who had surprised the audience in Antibes a few months earlier. Ina, at age 13, had won the Antibes International competition in France. Her score of 38.75 was just great! Agapova had won the Japanese Junior meet in Osaka with 38.95, so we see how close these two girls are.

The childlike Svetlana Agapova, with her sudden grin and big eyes, proved a great hit at Wembley in England, home of the huge World Cup matches in football as well as ice shows, boxing matches, and sports meets. This is where the gymnastics competitions are held when they are big internationals and only the very best perform. Svetlana was not the best girl there. Not at all. An

Galina Glutschenko *(Norbert Smyk)*

Elena Naimushina   *(Courtesy Novosti)*

English girl was before her, as well as an American first, a Romanian second and an East German third. But to see Svetlana perform is to feel happy and carefree. She does that to people. She looks so much as though she wants to please you that you work with her. She loves to hear the crowd clapping and, if you look closely, you will see her hide a small grin behind her hand as she runs off. If, and it happens, she does not do too well when she thought she would, her small flat face falls and the tears are very, very close. Her routine on the balance beam was not as graceful as it could have been, but she does try new things and hard ones. This was where the people loved her. That takes courage, they would say, and cheer, even if she fell. For it is often easier to perform routines everyone does well than to try something new and fail! Her vaults was second best overall, and so were her uneven bars. Floor exercise scoring was low for everyone and Agapova's 9.25 was only fair. She knew she had not done well and her jutting chin trem-

Ina Mitrofinova   *(Norbert Smyk)*

bled, but she held her shoulders back as she ran off. Courage must go hand in hand with a gymnast. You take the bad things with the good. And you tell yourself that tomorrow you will be better.

Earlier, the people had watched Svetlana on national television in the 1978 *Moscow News* competition. With above-average floor routines she had won a silver medal, plus another medal for placing third all around, behind Muckhina and Filatova. This was the meet in which the 14-year-old Naimushina was able to move up to seventh all around, showing that she is a threat for the future. Ina had beaten Svetlana Agapova in Vilnius. Agapova came in second all around, with another unknown, Marina Glotova, in third place. The young Elena Naimushina went into the senior group and did not do well. She came in thirteenth overall. In the finals many girls got the score of 10 plus; under the Russian scoring system a girl can get added points on top of the highest score of ten. This was something which Nadia brought about. Nadia was the first in international competition to get the magic number. After her, came others. Because it was too hard to give correct scoring for girls who did more difficult routines, the Russians said they were going to add to the 10.00 score. This meant that girls who were really super on the beam or bars could get 10.40 or 10.50 and up. In the Vilnius meets, Schidunova got a 10 plus score, Muckhina 10.20, Tereschenko 10.45 and, in floor exercise, Muckhina got a 10.60. In floor exercise, Ina Mitrofinova was fifth, even at age thirteen.

Against the Romanian juniors the Russian juniors lost the gold medal but won all the places. Glutschenko came in third and Agapova was fourth. A Russian called Fomitcheva was second and Romania's Dana Craciun was first. This shows that there are more good Russian girls coming up than there are good Romanian girls. Romania is a much smaller country and just does not have enough people. The Soviet Union has so many to choose from.

Elena Naimushina is coached by Valentin Shevchuk; she was his very first personal gymnast or what is known as a protégé. Nadia was, in a way, the protégé of Bela Karolyi. It means someone who is under the personal care of someone else. Well, Elena is somewhat like her similarly named associate—Elena Muckhina. They are both very solemn-looking girls with Elena Muckhina the more somber of the two. She is a bit darker also, as Naimushina is fair haired, with blue eyes. It has been said that Muckhina is very nervous and shy. She finds it very hard to smile during meets and this may be because she is afraid of mistakes or even the crowd and why she does better at home than away.

Tatiana Arshannikova is very new to the international scene. She is said to be the girl to replace Olga Korbut. She is assured and confident. Alas, there is no sign of the bright, flashing Korbut smile as yet! Both Tatiana and Elena Naimushina like the very hard tricks. And both are about the same age, so they compete with each other. Tatiana, aged fourteen, really showed her depth of talent at a meet with Czech, Polish, American, British and other European gymnasts taking part. The meet was won by Larissa Milovana, a real unknown. She scored 38.45 for the four events. Remember, no more than 10.00 was allowed for each event, for a total of 40.00, which is perfect. Tatiana was a very close second with 38.40, with great scores of 9.70, 9.70, 9.55, 9.45. Just about equal on everything! In the finals, Arshannikova won three out of the four events for two more medals—gold ones—to add to her silver! Then she got two more silver medals. All together she had two gold and three silver medals. What a gymnast! The Russians think very highly of her, and see her as one of their great stars of the future. The Olympics are not that far away now.

Tatiana is a person who is withdrawn. People wonder why she is looking so far away and they ask her. Tatiana always has a reply ready! One such reply is that she is listening to herself. Clever girl! She is also very talented. At one meet, she performed three double somersaults in her floor exercise—something very unusual. She is able to do the things both Olga and Nelli did in competition, even the Korbut loop. Naimushina likes to perform to Russian folk music, which makes the crowd very happy because they can hum along. Tatiana works just as hard as Elena, of course. She won the hearts of everyone present when she performed in the Soviet Youth Championships. She came second all around then, with Glutschenko third and Naimushina fourth. In the Dynamo Championships in Ostrava, she again came in second all around. Elena was the one who caught the eye in the USSR Championships in Tscheljabinsk, however. The 14-year-old came in a high third, right behind the top named Muckhina and Maria Filatova. In this competition, the popular Natasha Tereschenko was a lowly twelfth.

Natasha (or Natalia, which is another way of saying the same name—like Joan and Joannie) was the young gymnast who took New York by surprise in the American Cup. This was in early 1978,

Natasha Tereschenko   *(Norbert Smyk)*

and everyone expected the dark-eyed Shaposhnikova to win. Natasha lives in a small town called Ust-Omchug, which is in Magadan, some ten hours away from Moscow by airplane. This will show you how big their country is! Well, a few years ago they opened a gymnastics school there, with about two hundred young gymnasts. Here they tried to work and improve their talents. One of the coaches was a man called Eduard Nechai. Nechai found and worked with a slight, pretty girl called Tereschenko. It paid off, as we will see. She came in second in the All-Union School Spartakiade, behind Muckhina. People like Natasha because she has a warm, yet shy, smile. When she smiles, you feel warm too.

It is thought that Tereschenko is not really a fighter yet, like Grosdova. She does not always win. She likes to take part. She did enjoy the Junior National Championships in 1977, and she placed second all around. In that meet, she also won gold medals for floor exercise, beam and vault. Not bad for someone from a region as far north as Alaska! Maybe because she was so far away we did not hear about all the great things Natasha could do. It is said she was able to do the very hard vault-known as the Tsukahara with a full twist long before Nelli Kim did it. Her coach says that she is sometimes stubborn, which is good. One thing he says about her is that she does not like to be second best, which is not good. Everyone who competes tries to win, of course. But sometimes Tereschenko sees someone do a move she is going to do also, and she then loses interest. It could be that, if another girl has such a large lead over her in a meet, she feels there is no point in trying to catch up. This would account for the times she has been as far back as fifth or sixth against lesser-known girls. Her coach says that she shows great interest in learning something new, however. No matter how hard it is she has to work on it until she is able to do it the right way. In the last Junior Nationals this pleasant young lady did show them. She performed a Tsukahara vault with one and one-half twists. That really brought the crowd to its feet—a great moment for this girl from the RSFSR (Russian Soviet Federated Socialist Republic) Club.

Then came New York. No one took much notice of Tereschenko there. All eyes were on the girls from East Germany and Romania, as well as Shaposhnikova. This was good. Natasha was able to work on her own routines, without anyone bothering her. Shaposhnikova failed in the bars and beam events, so did not go into the finals. Lots of room for Tereschenko! Writers said that she was a very "exciting little gymnast." The crowd thought so, too, when she did her double back somersault off the beam. She also got the highest score for her work on the uneven bars, a 9.70. She did the hard moves with ease, showing her lovely arm movements. Natasha ended up as the American Cup winner of 1978.

We talked about Shaposhnikova and Muckhina before. Elena Muckhina may well have reason to be heavy-browed and keep to herself. Her mother died when she was quite young and Elena was brought up by her grandmother, which is hard on a young child. People who know her think this may be why she is frightened of noise and of competitions. This is something she will have to try and overcome if she is to go further in gymnastics. Right now she is in the tenth grade at school and works with coach Viktor Klimenko, whom she joined in 1974. Shy or not, she does like movies and popular music.

Natalia Shaposhnikova, like Nadia, still likes her dolls. She likes to follow the advice of other girls. She, too, is quiet, and she, too, can be stubborn. But she does what her coach wants. Her coach was Ludmilla's famous coach, V. Rastorotsky. She does ask about moves and does like to do them her way, but only because she has her own ideas. She suggests things to her coach and then waits to see what he has to say. He admits that she has very good ideas, which are new. Before Rastorotsky, she was under Gennadi Maleyev, so he may have had something to do with her having strong ideas about routines.

Natalia does not like to fail. She will show tears if she knows she has failed in a routine. But when she does well, those great dark eyes really beam with pleasure. She likes to compete against others and sees this as a challenge. She, too, is with the RSFSR Club.

One thing Natalia really loves is the audience. The crowd watching seems to set her on fire and brings out her great talent. She is one hundred percent a performer, an actress and a fine gymnast. She has been called "lyrical" by writers, the same word they used when talking about Tourischeva and Grosdova. Lyrical refers to a tender, joyous feeling—all of which sums up Natalia Shaposhnikova. At the 1977 World Cup, which was won by the superb little girl from Siberia, Maria Filatova, Natalia came very close to taking second place, even with the well-known East German Steffi Kraker, Marta Egervari of Hungary and Muckhina of the Soviet Union. Natalia was the big hit with everyone. They said that her every move was "beautiful." Judges liked her routines and gave her good scores. She was, by far, the most talked about gymnast there and one reason was a great routine on the uneven bars which they called "breathtaking." For this great performance, we

can thank another great lady, Ludmilla Tourischeva, who had helped coach Shaposhnikova.
Natalia's vaulting was nearly perfect, bringing her
scores like 9.75, and it was this event for which she
won the gold medal. When she came in behind
Steffi Kraker of the GDR, it was very very close—
38.20 to 38.45. Maybe next time. . . . After all, she
had beaten the girl from East Germany in the *Moscow News* competition earlier. In that, she had
come in second in both floor exercise and vaulting
for two silver medals and second in the all around
for another. Tereschenko was one of those "unofficial" gymnasts, who were not scored with the
rest. Had she been so scored, she would have
placed in an eighth place tie with several other
girls.

One thing which amused many who saw her was
the odd leotard which Natalia Shaposhnikova
wears. It is known in the United States as "tie-
dyed." This means it is a funny, blotchy, smudgy-
looking leotard. Some say it looks like a pink
leotard with dirty finger marks! Muckhina almost
always wears a leotard with daisies all over it.
Tereschenko has been wearing one-color leotards,
such as dark red. Agapova also has worn plain red,
or single colors.

Of the many other younger girls still coming up,
the ones they talk about most are Naimushina,
Mitrofanova, Arshannikova and the almost-un-
known Natalia Yurchenko. This latest Natalia (or
Natasha) is 14 years old and is a student of the
well-known Vladislav Rastorotsky. She is from
Rostov-on-Don. She looks quite a bit like Natasha
Shaposhnikova, who is from the same area. They
say she is very strong with very good coordination,
which is another way of saying that she is able to
make every part of her body work well with every

other part. Her program is full of hard moves, but it is said that Natalia Yurchenko is able to learn things quicker than other gymnasts.

The Soviets now have the pick of so many young girls whom they can add to their older teenagers, Svetlana Agapova and the two Natalias, Tereschenko and Shaposhnikova. With Nelli Kim, Maria Filatova and Elena Muckhina on the team, they should be really unbeatable. Nadia might win single titles, but the Soviets have the team strength. They demonstrated this in October 1978 when they dominated the world championships at Strasbourg.

The Russian people can be well pleased with their new young gymnasts, out of whose ranks they should easily find another Olga and Ludmilla. None will be quite the same as those two, of course. But, among the new girls, they will find new stars, who might even twinkle a little brighter, if in a different way.

Natalia Yurchenko   *(Courtesy Novosti)*

Chapter 4

Romania

Her name is Rodica Dunca. She is only 12 years old. When she was six she took her first gymnastics lesson. Nadia was the same age when she began. Rodica's club was called C.S.M. Baiai Mare and her trainer (coach) was Marinescu. Rodica was quiet, like Nadia, and kept to herself. But, when she performed gymnastics, she became happy. She knew this was what she wanted—and her trainer knew also.

Rodica is not yet comparable to Nadia. She did place third in the Romanian championships in 1976, when she was only ten years old, and, in the Balkan championships the next year, she won medals in beam and vault. This Romanian meet was in the master's category, not the national title. She had been on the winning team in the junior championships in 1974 also. 1977 was good to this daughter of a miner. She won the title in the third division in the Romanian nationals and the Romanian Cup in the second class or group. Her team also placed second. In the Balkan championships, Dunca won gold medals for her beam and vault routines. Not bad for someone only just past 11 years old!

Dumitrita Turner   *(Ion Mihaica)*

The young lady who won the Balkan championship in 1977 is Dumitrita Turner. She was born on the 12th of February in 1964 in a very famous place, Onesti, Nadia's home. Her teachers in gymnastics were Florica and Florin Dobre. She was seven when she first started. Later, Dumitrita beat out the girls from the Soviet Union to win that Balkan title. She went on in 1978 to become the schools champion of Romania in the masters category. This young girl worked very hard for her coaches and it paid off. In the International Championships of Romania, she rewarded them by winning both the floor exercise title and placing second all around.

Dumitrita did not do as well when she went to England in 1977. She tied for seventh place with an English girl and her only good score was a 9.35. To perform in a foreign country in front of strange people can make a young girl very nervous. Still, her gymnastic federation thinks highly of her for the future. They sent her to China in 1978 to represent Romania along with the great Nadia. The Chinese performed very well. They did better than anyone thought they would and ended up beating the Romanians. Turner even surprised herself. She was the very best girl there in floor exercise and she won a gold medal in this for her team!

In a meet against the Italians, Dumitrita did not do as well. She ended up in fourth place. The better known Marilena Neacsu was second, and Nadia won the meet. Rodica came in fifth, which was great because of her lack of competition against others. Rodica is too young even for the World Championships. Rodica is training with Nadia and Teodora in Bucharest in a training area there. The other two were scheduled for the World Championships in Strasbourg, but not Rodica. She has to wait until she is older. Nadia says that Rodica has a lot of patience in picking up new moves and ideas. Teodora also thinks very highly of Rodica. She thinks she is quick to learn, but says also that she is splendid and "very intelligent; I have never seen anyone who has made so much progress as she has at her age." Teodora trained with the best in the world, so this is great praise indeed.

One thing that many people have said about training in Onesti, was that it was much too hard for young girls. It was said that they had to eat what they were told and that they had very little because of dieting. Others who watched them training were shocked at what the coaches made the young girls go through. The Americans who saw said the girls were afraid to do anything without their coach telling them. Others said that it was so strict the girls never laughed or smiled and the young ones seemed like machines, only moving when told to.

Well, one can not say. This is all heard from others, and it may be that some young girls have to be told and to be directed. It made Teodora and Nadia two very great stars in world gymnastics. Maybe it *was* hard on them. All gymnasts have to train from four to six hours a day, five or six days a week. This is rough on any young girl. Of course, one does not have to train like this just to be a gymnast but only if one wants to become a world champion. This is why so many leave the sport when they get to be seventeen or eighteen years old. Not everyone loves it as much as others do.

Emilia Eberle is very slender, with fair hair and a thin face. Most Romanian girls are darker haired and have dark eyes, but not Emilia. There are times when she performs like someone very far away, her eyes seeing beyond. She does not seem to be a

Marilena Neacsu   *(Pete Huggins © Photofacts)*

fighter in competing against others. And Emilia is very fragile looking. She does not have a heavy body or thighs. She does have one thing most of the Romanian girls do not, outside of Teodora, a ready smile. The lack of smiles seems to be a part of the Romanian way of gymnastics. Most Romanian gymnasts look very serious and not too happy when they perform. This solemn-face idea makes some fans upset. They think Olga Korbut and Maria Filatova made people happy to watch them, and this is what gymnastics is all about. Even little Rodica Dunca does not seem to smile or even relax when she performs. So it is nice to watch Emilia.

Eberle is fourteen and has a lot of meets behind her. She proved very popular when she was in the United States in 1977. Emilia, who is very thin, gave a fine display on beam and was very good in all events. She was close behind teammate Nadia in the final standings. The people of Mexico also made Emilia their favorite when she toured that country the same year. They said her floor exercise was very beautiful.

Emilia does not seem to have the fighting instinct which helps gymnasts beat others. This was seen in the Chunichi Cup held every year in Japan. Although she had scores of 9.35 on floor exercise and 9.40 for her beam routine, she only placed thirteenth. Of course, she still has lots of time to get better. Emilia came in third in the Romanian Nationals in 1977, but Nadia and Teodora did not take part. However, in the 1978 Strasbourg world championships, with both the older girls competing, she did very well.

Gabi Gheorgiu is a sturdy girl. She has strong muscles and thick dark hair. She was born very near the Soviet Union in a town called Galati. It was not until she was eight years old that she joined a gymnastics club. This club was called Dunarea, and her coach was named Hustiuc. Gabi, who was born in September, 1963, was by then old enough to know that she liked this sport a lot. Little was heard of her, though, until she joined the club of Bela Karolyi in 1976. She was then aged 13. Because this was the year of the Olympics, not many competions were being held.

In 1977 Gabi was on the team that was in Orleans in France for the Orleans International. Nadia and Teodora finished first and second and the girl from Galati did very well to finish in third place. At the *Moscow News* meet, Gabi was set upon doing her very best against all well-known people, like Filatova, Kraker, Muckhina and so on. It was a big chore for a person new to the international scene. Gheorgiu need not have worried. She came in fifth all around—a great finish! The crowd loved her floor exercise, for which she got 9.40. Gabi did not do well in vaulting in Moscow or in Riga where the Riga Invitational is held. This was odd because Gabi held the Romanian vaulting title in 1977. Still, all gymnasts have off days and perhaps this was one for Gabi.

When she took part in the national championships of Romania she should have scolded herself, for she came in fifth all around again. Neither Nadia nor Teodora took part, so she did not have the better girls against her. This was not a good score for Gheorgiu. But Gabi was able to show what she could do when their team went to the United States. Some of the Romanian girls were very sloppy and gave funny, jerky displays on floor exercises. Their tumbling, apart from the great Nadia, was called poor to fair. Gabi gave a very strong beam routine, with a full twisting dismount, which is very hard to do. In fact, when they

Gabi Gheorgiu   *(Ion Mihaica)*

were in New York, one writer said that Gabi stole the show! He said that her routines were "unique." She also had the showmanship that made the crowd clap and cheer.

Gabi was able to show better what she could do when she went to Nagoya in Japan for the Chunichi Cup in November of 1977. She was not able to defeat the Soviet girls, not the East German, Kraker, but she was the best of the three Romanian gymnasts there. She ended up in fifth all around, a familiar spot for the dark-eyed Gheorgiu.

The Romanians have other fine young girls, of course, such as Neacsu, who had had a lot of competition in 1978, Marilena Vladauru and Christina Itu, who did very well in meets in Japan. Rodica Sabau and Mirela Oancea are young girls who have appeared in some foreign meets. Sabau scores over 9, but Oancea has a long way to go. Karolyi is working with the younger girls and people say it is only a matter of time before he has another Nadia.

The future for the Romanian girls is *always* good, because they start so young. The Romanian gymnasts are among the top three teams in the world today. Now that China has come into view, this may change the standings. But, millions of people hope that somewhere in that strange, unusual country there is another Nadia.

Chapter 5

Czechoslovakia

One cannot open *Sportovni Moderni Gymnastika,* the gymnastics magazine of Czechoslovakia, without seeing the likeness of Eva Mareckova. The pretty, long-haired girl, whose hair is usually tied back in a ponytail, is one of the finest Czech gymnasts. As far back as 1976, Eva was winning meets against the East German juniors when she was only 11 years old! Now she is a veteran of international competition, seen by all in the United States when she performed with great charm in the American Cup, and again from Japan, when she placed first in the 1977 Japanese Junior Invitational.

Mareckova, which is pronounced *Maretchkova,* is only 14 years old now, but already accepted as the best in Czechoslovakia. Her only real rival from her native land has been the very small solemn girl, Vera Cerna. She does not have the perfect skills that Nadia had at that age, but she is a girl with loads of talent, and a cheerful, if not shy, smile. Most of the Czech girls have been of more than usual good looks, and Mareckova, Larisa Milanova, Dana Brydlova and Tatiana Lickova are all among these. Not since the days of the world-famous Vera Caslavska has Czechoslovakia

Eva Mareckova   *(Glenn Sundby)*

had so many gymnasts with looks and talent. Caslavska, of course, was a world champion and she is now training her own daughter to follow in her footsteps.

Mareckova, Brydlova and Cerna are all 14-year-olds who are taking part more and more in the world's major meets. Cerna and Mareckova usually end up as rivals and one always seems to knock off the other for top place. These two could not be more unlike each other. Vera Cerna is the one gymnast who does not fit the "group." She is very very small and looks rather like a little boy with bows in his hair! Vera is straight up and down to look at, which makes her look more like a ten-year-old than fourteen. Speaking of ten-year-olds, Martina Pexova made the international scene early, when she took part in the Kiosice Invitational in 1977. She was then all of ten years old! Poland, Hungary and Britain were taking part also, but the Czech girls won every event. Jana Labakova was another ten-year-old who showed good moves, with poise. Neither Pexova or Cerna can see over the vaulting horse, and Cerna's trainer (coach), Sonya Hudeckova, has to bend way down to talk to her.

Like many of the Czech girls, Martina, Eva, Dana, Tatiana and Zelinkova all wear their hair in bangs or, as it is called in Europe, a fringe. They must find this good for gymnastics because it never gets in their eyes. Someone whom this harsh style does not suit is the rather plain little Cerna. Maybe, as she gets older, she will find something a bit prettier. Eva is able to wear any kind of hair style with *her* face.

Eva Mareckova was seen to be a great new talent as far back as 1976 when she took part in a meet against East Germany for 12- to 13-year-olds and

Vera Cerna *(Norbert Smyk)*

won very easily over everyone else. She did not do well in the *Moscow News* meet in 1977 but Dana Brydlova placed twelfth in actual scoring although, because of many ties, her final placing was listed as fifteenth. Eva did do better at Riga, placing twelfth in final standings, or tenth in scoring. As we said elsewhere, when there are several tied for one place, they count the number of places as one, two, three and the person who comes next is that many places further down. If Eva was behind three girls who all had the same score for a third-place tie, then she would be listed as in sixth place. They go by the number of girls ahead of her, and not by the score she made.

Eva still had not caught the public's eye in the international meets. The Russian girls and the East

Dana Brydlova *(Norbert Smyk)*

Germans were the ones who did. Vera Cerna, how-ever, despite her tiny body, did do quite well as did Dana Brydlova. Dana was to come in tied for elev-enth in the big European Championships in 1977, in which she had only one poor routine, floor. Vera came in eighteenth in this meet.

The annual Antibes Tournament in France was used as a stage for the younger gymnasts from dif-ferent countries. In 1977, the Soviet Union, East Germany and Czechoslovakia sent some of their newer talent along. The tiny Vera Cerna had one of her very best meets, coming off well in every event. Kraker and Gorbik tied for second place, and Vera came right after them. She did win a medal for third place on beam along with a French girl. It is very hard for Vera to be truly graceful because of her size. This means that many of her routines tend to be a bit jerky. Dana was able to place eighth all around in Antibes.

She was able to do a good double back somer-sault in her floor exercise in the Japanese Junior Invitational in 1977. Eva Mareckova did not win a medal although she did win another in Japan that year. In a meet known as the Dynamo Spartakiade, however, Eva was in top form. With young gym-nasts from Poland, the Soviet Union and many from all over Czechoslovakia, Eva still was able to win the title over the Russian, Arshannikova. By now people were getting a bit confused. Eva looks a lot like Natalia Tereschenko of the Soviet Union —they even have the same hairstyle!

The World Cup set the stage for another fine dis-play by Vera Cerna. This time Vera was able to move right up there with the very best— Shaposhnikova, Egervari, Kraker and Filatova. The year was 1977, when Vera was just 14. Her only low score was on balance beam, her others all over 9.45. In the single events she was able to win a silver medal for her floor exercise, beating (of all people) the lovely Natalia Shaposhnikova. This was a great night for this very small gymnast. When the Japanese Chunichi Cup came around, it was hard to decide who would win: Agapova, Kraker, Egervari, Shaposhnikova, Kunhardt, Trantow—all the very best of the world's young gymnasts. Vera was by far the shortest one there, looking all of 9 or 10 years old. Perhaps because of this, the Japanese were really taken with her. But she did not do anything really super, sad to say. Three girls came in tied for fourth place and, after them, in seventh place, came Vera. First place Agapova, second place Kraker and third place Shaposhnikova were all at their very best.

Meanwhile Jana Labakova was doing very well in her meets. For her age, it was quite astonishing. Labakova was entered in meets with the older thirteen- and fourteen-year-olds in 1977 and was able to get scores of 8.50 plus, as well as some in the low nines. Jana is with the club called Banik Ostrava. In the major meet, which Milanova (USSR) won, Jana came in a well-placed fourth in all around, beating out thirty-two other girls, including several Americans. She was doing so well that her club entered her in the Czech meet against the juniors from the German Democratic Republic. Jana, with her hair puffed up in two large bouncy ponytails tied with giant ribbons, was good enough to place third. In the Dynamo Spartakiade, she had tied for sixth with an East German girl. Then, some months later, she had entered the Youth Championship and, at the age of eleven, placed fifth in the all around competition.

Tatiana Lickova   *(© Volker Hischen)*

Moving up along with her was Tatiana Lickova (pronounced *Litchkova*). Tatiana had come in right on the heels of Dana in the *Moscow News* meets in 1977 and had ended in a high seventh spot in the Riga Invitational meet, above Eberle of Romania, Elfi Schlegel of Canada and Satako Okazaki of Japan.

In the 1977 Kiosce Invitational, a sprite of a girl made headlines. The youngest one of all, Martina Pexova, did some surprising things. The slant-eyed Pexova won a bronze medal for her beam routine and came in third in all around. What a great night for the ten-year-old, who is with TSM Litvinov Club under Hlinkova.

In the Czechoslovakian National Championships in 1977, the winner was the lovely Eva Mareckova, with 75.90 points. Vera Cerna, of Zbrojovka Brno, was second with 75.575 points and the veteran Ingrid Holkovicova was third. Tatania Lickoya was in fifth place. In the finals, Mareckova won two events and Vera Cerna won two, showing again how evenly matched these two young girls are. Lickova was second in one event and also won two bronze medals in the Nationals. Both Mareckova and Cerna topped the 9.70 mark in scoring in separate routines.

Vera was thought good enough to send to England for the major Champions All meet in 1978 and she tried hard to keep up with the other gymnasts but failed badly.

In the 1978 Antibes meet in France, Labakova was once again a firm favorite. She did well enough. She got a 9.60 for a vault routine, and finished eleventh all around. The tiny Czech could barely see that high, yet she was able to turn in another superb vault and finished in fifth place in the Orleans competition. That she was able to come from a lower finish to a higher one so quickly shows the promise in this youngster. As we will see, she was able to do very well in the 1978 Kiosce Invitational. In that competition, she came in fourth in vault, tied for third in bars and came in third in floor exercise.

The American Cup in 1978 saw both Vera Cerna and Eva Mareckova entered. Each girl wanted to do her best and, as always, each tried to do just that. Both performed the very hard double back somersaults to the delight of the huge crowd. At last, Vera could try her very best on beam. The sturdy little girl worked and worked. She threw everything into it. It paid off. A whopping 9.65 score was given her, for the highest in the finals! She also did well on the uneven bars, with a 9.40. Alas, she did not (yet again) look good in her floor exercise and got only 9.15.

Eva, meanwhile, was more solid in her routines. She was able to come up with sound scores each time, 9.55, 9.35, 9.30 and 9.45; these were good enough to bring her at last a bronze medal in international competition. The crowd likes her style and her dark, pretty looks. She smiles and looks as though she likes what she is doing. It was too bad that Shaposhnikova did not make the finals, but only because of the brilliance of teammate Tereschenko.

The 1978 Czechoslovakian National Championships were held in Prague. To no one's surprise they were again won by Eva Mareckova. Her score of 75.625 gave her the title over Cerna, with 74.325, and Radmilla Zemanova. Brydlova was fifth and Lickova was sixth all around, again showing how close all these young girls are, although there was quite a distance in actual points scoring. Labakova did not take part in this championship meet, so it is hard to say where she would have finished.

Looking at them again, it would seem that Labakova, Pexova, Lickova, Cerna, and Brydlova will join Mareckova as the best in Czechoslovakia. They are all getting better all the time and, because of their age, they must always improve. The United States got a look at some of the young Czechs when they competed in Arizona and put on an exhibition in New Mexico. This was one time when the girls from the land of the dollar did very well for themselves. They put on a great show to take all of the first four places. Eva Mareckova was the best Czech girl, coming in fifth. Labakova came in a lowly eleventh in the all around standings. The scoring was not high, with Eva's points total only 36.90. Radmilla Zemanova placed eighth, yet in a meet with young Romanians she was able to win the title. This showed the progress of the Americans in comparison to the Romanians.

The Czechs are always trying and always enjoy their own performances. The young girls always have a smile and, while not always as graceful as their lovely countrywoman, Caslavska, give as much pleasure as they can to the audience. One day, it may lead to the gold medal.

Chapter 6

The German Democratic Republic

The teams of East Germany or the German Democratic Republic (GDR) have for a very long time had some of the finest gymnasts in the entire world. From Annelore Zinke through Karen Janz, they reigned through the 1960s and part of the 1970s. Today, they still have some of the very best gymnasts available anywhere.

Regina Grabolle is now only 12 years old. Yet, a year ago, she was able to do a double somersault with ease. Another young gymnast, when 14, was able to do a triple twist in floor exercise as well as from the uneven bars. Jana Wierbinski is said to be about the only one who can do this trick. Strange as it seems, she does not win in the meets she has entered. It may be that she is a specialist in certain events only. Jana is from Halle in Germany. She did do well in the Youth & Children's Spartakiade in 1977 when she came in second to Franka Voigt. Although she was the national children's champion in 1976, she has not yet made the jump to the older age group in the terms of winning.

Steffi Kraker *(Norbert Smyk)*

The best-known two girls from the German Democratic Republic are Steffi Kraker and Silvia Hindorff. Steffi is the big winner or, at the very least, she usually places in meets. Silvia is another who has come to the fore very very quickly. She is getting more popular all the time.

In 1977, the East German National Championships saw the 12-year-old Regina Grabolle in third place. Regina was then only four feet eight inches tall. Another time, when her country met the Swiss team, Regina was able to win the title, with Silvia third and Ina Koppe sixth. Ina is the daughter of Erwin Koppe, who was a German gymnast and champion.

The pouty Sigrid Trantow was a hot favorite in 1977 but was injured and, because of this, she has not been active. But she has won meets against Norway and Sweden. Another girl who started very well, but somehow got lost amidst all of this talent, is Heike Kunhardt. Heike does not have the number of foreign meets she needs to help her gain more experience. Somehow Silvia has been able to come from nowhere and zip into all the main meets! She has much more appeal than Heike and her fair beauty has all the photographers begging for more pictures.

Heike was very active in 1977 in Germany. Her short, somewhat stocky build helped her in events where muscle power was needed. In the European Championships, she was able to defeat the classy Steffi Kraker, ranked number one. In that meet, Heike was seventh all around. Not that good, granted, but this was the famous meet in which all the best women in the world took part—Nadia, Nelli Kim, Muckhina, Egervari, Filatova and so on. To come seventh in that company was a great feat. Her scores were good, from the 9.65 on bars down to the 9.50 on vault. In the single events or, as they are known, the individuals, Heike was beaten out by Steffi in vault and, oddly enough, on bars. In floor exercise, Heike was able to beat out Steffi. In the French Antibes tournament, Heike placed sixth all around, below what she is able to do. After that, possibly because of injury, young Fraulein Kunhardt faded from sight rather quickly. Up and coming young Germans took her place, among them being Silvia, Jana and Sigrid Trantow, back after her injury.

Heike Kunhardt   (© *Alan E. Burrows)*

Sigrid Trantow *(Fritz Giessler)*

Ina Koppe has a round, childlike face, but is able to express a good deal more than childishness in her floor exercise. She is a very fine young gymnast. She is able to perform very hard routines, and does an exciting dismount from the uneven bars. This dismount is known as a piked front twist from the low bar, coming to stand facing it. She has several dismounts that vary and some are much harder than others, of course. Her piked dismount involved a half a twist around the bar with a longways motion, into a piked somersault to bring her to a standing pose facing the bar.

Silvia Hindorff is the only girl who comes close to filling the shoes of either Angie Hellman or Gitta Escher. These girls were so beautiful and so graceful that everyone envied them. When Angelika danced, the watchers wanted to dance also! Almost all of the Olympic team of 1976 retired within two years. This meant that the German Democratic Republic had to find suitable girls— fast.

The GDR has a wonderful sports system. It is one of the best in the whole world. All children can take part and the government gives them the training, the teaching, the things to perform on. More than 5,000 people are teaching gymnastics in the German Democratic Republic. The schools have gymnastics programs, the youth clubs have gymnastics, the companies that employ people have gymnastic clubs, and church groups have gym clubs. As you can see, the Germans are very sports-minded people. Because of this, the young girls are able to learn quickly and get free tuition. If they do not like one sport, they can go into another one.

In the Canadian Coca-Cola meet in 1977, Silvia Hindorff was third in scoring, placing fourth because of a tie for second between the USSR's Galina Glutschenko and Anka Grigoras of Romania. She did not enter the *Moscow News* meet, this being left to Steffi and Ina, along with newcomer Dagmar Schreiberg. Ina did have a very fine competition, however, coming in a tie for eighth place, with Steffi in fourth. Ina was even in better form in Riga in 1977, right after Moscow. In this she was able to come so close to Steffi that she almost took third place. It ended with a score of 37.35 for Steffi in second, with Yudina in third from the Soviet Union, with 37.15. Right behind was Ina Koppe with 37.10. Everyone gasped when they saw Ina's dismount from the uneven bars. Dagmar was then 16 years old, but not that good. The Japanese were able to see the girls from East Germany in 1977 at their Chunichi Cup. In this Heike, Steffi, and Sigrid Trantow were the three entered. While Steffi was in great form to come in second, Heike was a dismal twelfth, right behind Sigrid in eleventh place. Both had very low beam scores.

In 1977, a strange, homely girl came into the picture. She was Karen Casper—sporting huge bows in her hair. Maxi Gnauck, aged 13, also started to take part in more meets, but not too many because of her age. Maxi was in the big Spartakiade, held in Leipzig. This was won by Franka Voigt, and Maxi came fifth. Both girls did very well against the young Czechs in 1977, when they came in first and second with amazing scores—38.10 and 37.90. The judges must have been feeling in a very good mood that night! In a junior meet, the scores are usually in the 36-point range, up to 37. The winner of the 1978 Spartakiade was Kirsten Klotzek, about whom nothing much is yet known.

Karen Casper was chosen to go to the American

Cup in New York in 1978. She is an amiable girl
and likes people. In the opening day's meet, Karen
did something not expected at all. She beat Donna
Turnbow as well as Britain's Karen Robb to move
into twelfth place. Her best event was balance
beam. She did not go into the finals as only eight
girls were chosen for that last day. One who did do
so was another surprise. Her name was Birgit
Suesz. Birgit is one of the many unknown to the
rest of the world. She did so well at the New York
meet that she tied Eva Mareckova of Czechoslovakia for sixth place in the first day's meet and
came in sixth in the finals. She is a good tumbler
and very strong in floor exercise, with nice moves.

Canada, as we said before, greeted Silvia Hindorff in their Coca-Cola competitions. She looked
best in the uneven bar event in Ontario. She swung
a fine routine, for a high score. In Alberta, however, Silvia did not do that well in bars. Instead she
won a medal with the older Grigoras, for first place
on the balance beam. Silvia seemed to be getting
better as she went along and, as if to prove this, she
was sent to England for the Champions All competition in 1978. Her federation judged her good
enough also to send to Moscow and Riga.

How did Silvia do? Great! She was as pretty as a
picture, with her pink skin and lovely blonde hair.
She barely missed a fourth place finish in Moscow,
nosed out by American Rhonda Schwandt. She
came in fourth in vault, bars and beam. She did go
one better on floor and won a bronze medal for her
routine. Over in Riga, she slipped a little on beam
but managed to do well enough in the other events
for a bronze medal in all around. She swung well
for her bar routine and got a silver medal. She performed a fine floor routine and for that took an-

Silvia Hindorff   *(Alan E. Burrows)*

other silver medal. You could say that she had a good night overall!

The English liked what they saw when Fraulein Hindorff appeared there. They thought she was very elegant with a lot of style. Her scores were all good, except, oddly enough, for floor exercise. But they were good enough to win her a bronze medal over Agapova, Ovari and Cerna. Not bad company to be in!

Regina Grabolle has a lot of style for her age, barely 13, which is pretty young in any sport. Regina won a meet against Switzerland in 1977 and is said to be the *wunderkind* of East German gymnastics. This is a term given for any youngster who is great in his sport; it translates as "miracle child" and means an infant prodigy. Regina is still too young to be accepted in major international meets, but there is no doubt we shall be hearing lots about her very soon. She has great talent and this small dark girl reminds one of the marvelous gymnast, Annelore Zinke, who was forced to retire due to an accident. (Annie has since come back into the sport, we hear.)

Everyone who has seen her raves about Regina. They saw she has the ability of a more mature gymnast and her moves are quite outstanding. Also touted is Jana Wierbinski, who was a champion in the children's category. Jana is said to risk great difficulty in her routines and is always willing to try out even the hardest. She has done the triple twist from the high bar, which is breathtaking to watch (and scary, too). Her landing lacks polish yet, but just the fact that she can do a trick like this is amazing.

Silvia, Dagmar, Ina, Karen, Regina and Jana are all very fine gymnasts. These little *frauleins* are a

Regina Grabolle *(Norbert Smyk)*

great tribute to the fine sport system of the German Democratic Republic, which is hard at work rebuilding its once great Olympic team, of Hellman, Kische, Zinke, and others. It would appear they have every chance of being world contenders again, very very soon.

Chapter 7

The Peoples Republic of China

The place was Shanghai in China; the year 1978. All the seats in the huge stadium were filled. There was a deathly hush among the stands as all eyes were upon a lone figure, swinging with real ease, yet doing the hard tricks, on the uneven bars. When she came into her dismount, she knew she had done well. The crowd cheered! What a great performance they had seen! This was the night when Nadia Comaneci of Romania was in town. This was the night when the great Romanian team would surely take all honors in this first Shangai Invitational.

The girl turned and smiled as she ran off. Nadia, you ask? No—her name was Yen-Hung Ma and she was a fourteen-year-old Chinese schoolgirl! And what did she get in the way of a score for this great routine? Why, a 9.95! She was the star of the night. Nadia had been suffering with a heel injury, so only took part in team competition. Little Miss Ma knew the same feeling that Nadia had had when the Romanian was only fourteen—the joy and excitement of having done well and having the crowd warm to your efforts.

Mainland China Infants

The girls from mainland China are very new to the world scene. Before 1977, they kept within their own country. Now, they have at last joined the international world of gymnastics and are doing well. Young boys and girls are giving great performances, doing very hard tricks with ease.

Yen-Hung is tiny, but very quick and nimble. She tumbles very well and, of course, loves the uneven bars. She is ranked among the very best in China. They say there are many even better than she. There is an A team and a B team. Six members of the A team scored over 37.35 up to 39.00 points. Remember, the highest score for each event is 10.00, and hardly anyone ever gets that. This means that for all four events, the highest possible score would be 40 points. The B team has 4 girls who are able to score from 37.45 to 37.40 points, which means that every one scored more than 9.00 in any event.

Wen-Chu Ma *(Pete Huggins)*

Another Miss Ma, this time Wen-Chu, was the winner in vaulting. This was the little girl who did so well in England a few months earlier. The balance beam was won by a 16-year-old student, Cheng Chu. She is very beautiful and has long graceful legs and arms. She also likes to wear bows in her dark hair. Wen-Chu is from the province of Shanghai and she won a silver medal in the 1977 national championships. The Chinese women, as we can see, are all very good. Their gymnastics are the old style, with lots of grace and beauty. They have been seen on American television, and they really caught the fancy of the TV personnel. Too often they had seen bouncy acrobatics, which lacked beauty. Now they were seeing a classic style.

If we go back through the years, we find that more than 3,000 years ago the Chinese were already performing acrobatics and physical training. They believed this helped their bodies breathe and was good for the health of the person. They were able to do really hard tricks with their bodies, and even to do contortions. This word means they were able to tie their arms and legs into strange knots! Sometimes they could place their two feet behind each ear and walk on their hands. This was because so many over the years had become "double-jointed." Everyone has the same number of joints in their bodies, but the Chinese were trained to be able to move two ways instead of just one. This made them very popular as circus acts and they used to tour the world. Today we know them to be great acrobats and gymnasts. They are able to go a long way in sports because their government provides them with free teaching in their sports schools. The parents are asked if they want their child to go to sports school, if the coaches see that she has enough ability to go further. No money is charged if she does go. Ages run from seven years old on up. Most seem to be from ten to twelve years old in the sports schools, where they average three or four hours of gymnastic training each day. They also study forms of moves and ways to improve their dancing in the evenings. Although the equipment they have in most gyms is old, there is plenty available for all. As we said, they do not have to pay for anything. The state gives it all to them, as it believes that sports helps to make for a happy people.

The Chinese federation has asked to enter the International Gymnastic Federation and, once it is accepted, it is felt that they will soon become the next world champions—both men and women. The girls are a very cheerful, happy bunch. They seem to enjoy what they do and to like to perform in front of others. All have hobbies, of course.

Chinese Gymnasts in Training

Ya-Chun Liu *(Pete Huggins)*

Wen-Chu is a high school student; she is fifteen. She says she likes the vault best of all the events. Ya-Chun Liu is their national all around champion. She won the all around title in the Shanghai meet also. Miss Liu was third in the Nationals in 1976, when she was thirteen, and had grown so much better by 1977 that she won the title for the first time. When she was in Britain in 1977 she placed fifth all around. She is taller than the rest and very beautiful. She likes to wear her hair drawn back in a fall, with a huge bow. Her body is long and slender, and full of grace.

National team member Hsiao-Li Tang is another pretty girl, whose hair is styled in the Czech style, with a bang or fringe. She, too, has long slim legs, with graceful hands. Hsiao-Li is a sixteen-year-old from the Shansi province. She came in fifth all around in the 1977 national championships. She is a student in Peking, studying physical education—a very good choice. She does very well on the vault and bars, but is good in every event. She proved this by winning the meet in England against the British girls. She also was able to place first in Peking in 1977 in a match against Canada. Miss Tang prefers the vault over the other events. This is her second year on the National team.

Another sixteen-year-old won the balance beam title in Shanghai. Her name is Cheng Chu. She has a small face, with lovely slanting eyes. Her hands and feet are dainty, and her legs would be a movie star's delight. She is from Northern China, where she is a student. She was sixth in their national championships. Of all the events, Cheng says she likes the uneven bars the best.

The Chinese teams are so very strong that they

Hsiao-Li Tang *(Pete Huggins)*

Cheng Chu   *(© Alan E. Burrows)*

were able to send different teams to different meets. One success was in Canada in 1978. Wen-Chu Ma was the top performer in the Edmonton Pacific Rim meet, defeating American, Canadian and Australian gymnasts. The U.S.A.'s Christa Canary came in second, but Yung-Hsien Chen came in third for the bronze medal. Miss Chen is aged fifteen and is from the Hunan province. She came in fourth all around in their last national championships.

The favorite pastime of Wen-Chu Ma is reading and this is also a hobby of Hsiao-Li Tang and Ya-Chun Liu. Ya-Chun likes music and so does Cheng Chu. In many ways, they are very like their young American counterparts. When they were in Canada, they attended parties and were guest of honor at different dinners. They laughed and talked to people through the interpreter and were very friendly. The old-style heavy garments they used to wear in sports have given way to lovely modern leotards. Some of these leotards are sprinkled with daisies and are very becoming to the black-haired Chinese.

The girls to watch would seem to be the two Miss Mas! Cheng Chu and Ya-Chun Liu seem to be among the favorites of the Chinese federation also. They have many more younger ones who have not been seen outside China, of course. There is no question they will soon be competing against the Soviet Union for the world title. That will be a great battle to watch when it comes!

Chapter 8

The United States of America

Within each of the fifty states there is a gymnastics association under which clubs and groups organize. Every one has to belong to the US Gymnastics Federation if they wish to hold USGF meets within their state, but there are many private clubs which do not. There is also the US Association of Independent Clubs, which has many members and also holds gymnastics competitions. As with the USGF, many of these meets are sponsored by businesses. These sponsors help a great deal with the expenses of holding meets and, in return, they get free advertising and publicity.

The USGF invites foreign teams to tour the country and is the organizer of the well-known American Cup. It governs the judges, committees and groups which work within the USGF. In 1978, it agreed to make the Dial Soap people its partner in promoting gymnastics and staging events in the United States. Other such sponsors in the USA are Sears Roebuck, which works with the Amateur Athletic Union; Danskin, a leotards and gymnastics apparel manufacturer; AMF American and the Nissen Corporation, both equipment manufacturers. These are among companies which have helped gymnastics by staging or copromoting meets.

The American Cup (now known as the Dial-American Cup) is the biggest meet in the United States for foreign competitors. It has been lucky for American girls also; they have been winners or runners-up. Kathy Johnson and Donna Turnbow were first and second in 1977, and Kathy was second in 1978. Somehow this meet never had the impact that the foreign ones had. The American girls would enter the Moscow News or the Riga Cup and end way down at the bottom. They would go into the Champions All in England and not get a place. This all changed in 1977. Something wonderful happened to American gymnastics. The bad luck which had dogged the Americans in Europe was broken and they started to win! Let us have a look at the winners who are among the younger gymnasts.

The beginning of the American move up seems to have been the spring of 1977 with the Champions All meet in England. This is where the little girl from North Dakota, Robin Huebner, placed third. She beat Elena Davydova of the USSR and Sakiko Nozawa of Japan for this bronze medal. Robin was then sixteen years old. Like Kelly McCoy, who was only the second to get a perfect score of 10.00 in the USA, Robin has not been in that many major meets. Kelly scored her 10.00 back in 1976 but has not been a winner of major meets during the past years. Kelly was with the Christian gymnastic club called TWIGS when she did her great vault in the USGF Junior Nationals. She was then aged twelve.

One of the girls in this meet was a Merilyn Chapman, who was later to startle the world with some medal-winning routines in Europe. Merilyn was third all around in the 1976 Junior Nationals. She was then fourteen years old. Even then she was seen as a "great gymnast dealing with top difficulty," meaning she was able to work very hard moves into her routines. This was an Olympic Games year so there were few international meets held and, in most, the older girls were competing.

In the 1977 Championships of the USA, the older girls easily held on to win. Donna Turnbow and Kathy Johnson were followed by Lisa Cawthron, a toothy, amiable fifteen-year-old from Texas. Lisa had something in common with McCoy and a newly emerging group of young Americans—she was a top vaulter. In this national championship, Merilyn was well down in eighth place, but she did get a third place in vault in the individuals. In the Far West Invitational meet, Merilyn, from the Diablo Club of Jim Gault, was able to defeat the top-ranked Donna Turnbow to place first all around, as well as win the balance beam title.

Lisa was ranked well, following her all around win in the second National Elite tournament early in 1977. In sixth place in that meet was a young lady from Illinois, Christa Canary, a name to remember not only because it is pretty. Another junior meet of great value in rating gymnasts was the USGF Junior Nationals of 1977, which saw another name soon to make headlines—Rhonda Schwandt of California. This was Rhonda's first year in Class 1, so her third-place finish was of note. The big winner was Kari Lewis, a sparkling blonde from the Arizona Sunrays Club. A four feet ten bundle of energy, Kari was then only thirteen years old, so not ready for international competition.

Another name to watch was that of Gigi Ambandos, whose dark brown hair and dark eyes were in great contrast to the very blonde Kari. Gigi came in second all around and won both balance beam and floor exercise. Gigi was with the Parkettes Club of Allentown, Pennsylvania. She had a lot of class and elegance not seen in that many of the younger performers. She was marked down as someone with a future, although only thirteen years old.

The United States has two gymnastic bodies which have national as well as Olympic events. These are the USGF and the AAU, the Amateur Athletic Union. There are the USGF Junior Olympics as well as the AAU Junior Olympics. The word "nationals" only means that these meets are open to the whole of the United States, unlike "regionals," which are meets for those gymnasts in a given region or area. One can only have an international meet if there are girls from foreign countries taking part. Foreign girls cannot take part in national meets.

At the 1977 USGF Junior Olympics, in Oregon, the girl from the happily named Sunrays of Arizona, Kari Lewis, had a clear lead to place first all around. Although she had sore ankles, Kari was able to win the balance beam and floor exercise titles also. The thirteen-year-old's favorite performer is Nadia, so she may be hoping for as great a future as the Romanian.

One of the great losses to American gymnastics in 1977 was that of Stephanie Willim, who easily won the National AAU Elite Championships and seemed destined to be one of the greats. A back ailment made the young star cut short her exciting career, a sad thing indeed for the sport.

The AAU's Olympic meet for juniors was another battle between a blonde and brunette, as Lisa Nevill from Indiana won the all around over the "Texas Tornado," the nickname of El Paso's Pam Lee. The twelve-year-old Lee, as daintily blonde as the other girl was prettily dark, was fourth all around in the USGF Olympic meet.

Summer gave way to fall in America and with it came the girls from Romania—and Nadia. That was when fate took a hand in American gymnastics. Several American girls took part in a competition against the Romanians, and when it was over a "first" had taken place. Donna Turnbow had shared the uneven bars title with Nadia! Nadia had not done too well overall. She was thought by some watchers to have been scored too highly with even the 9.60 vault and bars she had been given. They said that Donna's routine was better and she should have been a clear winner. Either way it showed that at last the United States had grown up as far as competition was concerned.

The Americans competed in the World Cup in Oviedo, Spain, but it was a sad night for one girl when she forgot to change the number of the vault. That unhappy girl was the Texan, Lisa Cawthron, whose 9.70 vault was equal to that of Filatova. She forgot that the next time she was to have changed the number of the vault, which is required by the F.I.G. rules. This great vault of Lisa's was given a lower score as a result and pushed her further down in the standings. She did finish eighth all around, nonetheless.

Americans were still not doing too well abroad. They were always running behind the Russians, Romanians or Hungarians. It seemed as though the youthful "Yanks," as Europeans called them, were not going to win the big medals unless the other top gymnasts did not compete. Well, that was in 1977, and it seemed as though the year would end that way. But, in December, the fresh cool English weather brought good luck to the young American gymnasts. The meet was the new British Invitational, in which the USSR had sent Elena Gurina, Olga Koval and Valery Schidunova. Judit Mueller, Eva Kanyo and Horacsek came from Hungary. Others were over from Poland and Canada to compete against the local British girls.

As usual the crowd expected the Russians and the Hungarians to win. The meet was in the seaside town of Brighton, known for its salty air and great weather. It helped Merilyn Chapman, as we will see. Linda Kardos and Kelly McCoy were the other American gymnasts taking part. Vaulting was a surprise in that Kelly only got a 9.0 after taking steps upon landing. The first two girls managed to

Merilyn Chapman   *(Tom Wakeling)*

total 18.55 to tie the Russians. Kelly muffed her bars also for a 9.20 but the girl from the Diablo Club, Merilyn Chapman, hit a superb 9.55 routine, which tied the US team with the Hungarians. Linda did well on the beam for a 9.40, and Merilyn 9.35, which gave them the win in that event. All were going great in the floor exercise, with Linda at 9.45 and the other two eights at 9.50 each. The USA again led the field in that event. After the first night Merilyn led over everyone else. But could she hold on to that narrow lead? The young Americans waited with every nerve on end as they went into the second day of competition. Merilyn tied Gurina in vault with 9.20, Kelly managed a 9.30, and Linda a 9.10. Bars again was a high point for Merilyn as she was given a great score, 9.60; but Linda blew her dismount for a 9.00. Kelly did well to get a 9.35. The Russians both had bad routines for scores in the eights. Balance beam held the day for the visitors from the United States. By the end of the meet, Merilyn Chapman had won the floor exercise along with Kelly, as both scored a top score of 9.55

The final result was that Merilyn Chapman had placed first all around to win the gold medal and the title. Kelly McCoy came in third for the bronze behind Mueller of Hungary. The girls and their coach, Jim Gault, were thrilled. This was a great and moving moment for them all—to have won a title in a foreign country at long last! Great days for the USA! But at the end of the year no American gymnast was listed among the world's top ten women.

Merilyn Chapman, the worthy winner of the British Invitational, was born in April, 1962 and started tumbling when she was a five-year-old. She did not start in gymnastics until she was eight. By 1971, she was a beginner-novice and, by 1972, Merilyn was able to improve enough to take fourth all around in both regional and state meets.

In 1973, she was really going well, and to no one's surprise she won the state championship title. That year she had bad luck in the form of a broken elbow. Merilyn took it as only she can, with acceptance. She knew now she would lose months of hard work and would have to make it up. She was out of action most of 1974 because of this. Then, she bounced back. In 1975, she was able to come in second in the all around in the state championship when she was thirteen. In the Junior Nationals (USGF) she had placed fourth all around. In 1976, Merilyn was third in the state meet, after being first in the regionals. She was also third in the USGF Junior Nationals. Her big win that year was when she won the all around title in the USGF Junior Olympics.

So far, she had been too young for foreign competition, but she was doing fine against her countrywomen. In 1977, Jim Gault entered her into as many meets as he thought she was able to cope with. Regionals brought her third all around; National Elite Qualifying Round, also third all around and, finally, in the US Elite Championships, she was eighth all around. In the USGF National Junior Team selections, she was first-place qualifier and she easily won the Far West Invitational. She was now thought to be able to handle foreign competition, and Jim Gault was proved right when she placed first, second and third all around in various meets held in New Zealand. Merilyn was on the move!

She knew now that she could compete with even

the best-known gymnasts of the world. When the Czechoslovakians came to tour the United States, bringing with them their popular young champion, Eva Mareckova, Marilyn was not put off. Although her all around score was not hair-raising, she was still able to end up in first place, with Linda Kardos second, and Kelly McCoy third. The perky Jackie Cassello, daughter of the well-known gymnast, came in along with Mareckova in fourth place. This was the meet which paved the way for the three girls to compete in England.

During 1978, Merilyn entered the National Junior Elite Championships in Garden Grove, California. From Walnut Creek, California, Merilyn felt much at home in her own state. She was able to pick up the first all around medal, followed by Linda Kardos and Rhonda Schwandt, who had come in second in a meet against Japan a month earlier. Merilyn was now ready to take on Europe on any terms they wished to offer.

Joining teammates Schwandt and Kardos, Merilyn set forth for Russia and the *Moscow News* meet. She knew this drew most of the best gymnasts in the world, but she was going to try. Her teammates felt just the same way and, with them even more than with Merilyn, their trying paid off. Merilyn performed well, but just not well enough to place higher than fourth in any event. She was still able to beat out the highly touted Elena Naimushina of the USSR to capture sixth place in the all around. All her scoring was above 9.35 in all around.

Then they went to Riga and here Merilyn was able to pick up her first medal, when she placed third in floor exercise. She was not dismayed, though, as her teammates had been able to do very

Rhonda Schwandt   *(Tom Sauters)*

well with medals, as we shall see. Spurred on by the success of London, Rhonda Schwandt was out to prove what she could do against the best there was —and *how* she did it! The girl with the big smile and the bobbed short hair was like a bird let free at last. Rhonda became the first American to win a gold medal in international meets in the Soviet Union.

Rhonda was a girl who had come up really quickly. Before 1978, she had only been noted for her success in Orleans, France, when she came in second all around in the International Schools Gymnasiade. In that meet, she had also won floor and vault titles. A member of Dick Flood's Jetes Club, Rhonda was born in April, 1963, in Long Beach, California. Another world-famous gymnast came from the same area, the great Cathy Rigby. Young Miss Schwandt was only fourteen at the time she competed in Russia. Let us look at what this four feet eleven dynamo achieved over there.

The crowd had little interest in the young Americans, who were not expected to do well by anyone. After all, the famous stars Filatova, Muckhina, Agapova and Hindorff were all there. Surely they would win everything. Then along came Schwandt. Beaming at everyone, she bounded out to do her stuff. Uneven bar was the first event in Moscow for the Americans. Wham, bam, up went Rhonda! Her 9.55 was good, but not good enough to defeat Filatova and Muckhina. The Russians heaved a sigh of relief. For a moment—just a moment, mind you—they had been worried.

The other events saw Rhonda do fairly well, but she was not great until it came to vault. Then she was off into space! A wonderful vault got a good score, a 9.70. She performed what is known as a layout Tsukahara, a very hard vault. At the end of the first day, Rhonda was in third place, to the surprise of almost everyone. Only two girls from each country could compete in the finals so, when it came to the vault, Muckhina and Filatova were there for the Soviet Union. Rhonda knew she had her work cut out for her.

Neither of the Russians were able to give good enough vaults as both put their hands down on their full twists. Rhonda, however, was able to get a 9.45 as well as a 9.70. This meant the gold medal for the American girl at last! How excited she and her teammates were. Could they pull off any more medals on the other events? They surely would try. The uneven bars saw Filatova and Muckhina finish one, two, but right behind in third place with 19.10 was none other than Rhonda. Thus came a bronze medal for the young Californian.

The Soviet girls are great on balance beam, but even they make mistakes. Maria managed 9.55 and 9.65, and Elena Muckhina only 9.65 and 9.35. This was good enough to bring them the first two places, but hanging in there was Rhonda, with 9.25 and 9.30, to give her yet another bronze medal! She was doubly thrilled when she was given a special gift for being the outstanding foreign gymnast in the whole meet.

From Moscow the girls went to Riga. Although they were tired, the girls wanted to add more medals. Once again, Rhonda was up against the best; this time, the fine Natasha Tereschenko. Natalia won the vault title, but Rhonda came in second for the silver medal. She came in fourth in beam, but was not good enough to win a medal. Merilyn had added hers, a bronze for her floor work. Two medals were okay, and Rhonda had finished fourth all around behind the German, Silvia Hindorft.

Yet another meet loomed ahead. This was in Hungary, the big Hungarian Invitational. The Russians were missing from this meet, which made it much easier for the American girls. Zsuzsa Kalmar and Eva Ovari were the big guns for the Hungarians, but the United States had its own big gun with Rhonda Schwandt. Once again she was in top form to take the first place in vault and second in bars and, believe it or not, also in floor exercise! Rhonda did not do well in the beam, however, and finished fourth. Her 73.60 gave her third place in the all around, for a total of one gold, two silver, and a bronze medal! This fine little gymnast had won two gold medals, three silver medals, and three bronze medals in the three meets in which she had taken part in Europe. With Linda Kardos also getting bronze medals for vault and bars, it was a wonder the Americans were able to stagger home under all the weight of metal!

Rhonda is a cheerful girl who likes to swim and ride horses. She also likes art and perhaps this is why she is so artistic in her gymnastic displays. Merilyn is another bright person who, although she misses a lot of school because of gymnastics, still manages to get a high average. These two girls are certainly among the United States' best gymnasts.

Another 16-year-old is Christa Canary from Northbrook, Illinois. With the team of Bill Sands, called Mid-America Twisters, she, too, has come a long way very quickly. Christa was born in Iowa and did not start gymnastics until her parents had moved to Houston, Texas. She was then ten. She later moved to Chicago to train under Leonard Isaacs and began to train under her present coach,

Bill Sands, in 1975. Bill set up his own club in 1977.

Christa was vaulting champion in her age group as far back as 1975 and has been AAU Junior Olympic Champion and Senior Midwest Open Champion. She was still way down the list in major meets, such as Championships of the USA, although she did manage a first-place all around finish in the 1977 National Elite all around.

In 1978, Christa suddenly became noticed. "Who is she," people asked when Christa appeared on the international scene. Christa soon showed them! She was seen on television in the Championships of the USA. Her third-place all around was startling to many as she had so soon arrived on the elite scene. Ahead of her were the experienced Kathy Johnson and Donna Turnbow. Right behind her was Kelly McCoy and another newcomer, Marcia Frederick.

Christa turned in fine routines on vault (third place) and bars (second place) to add to her bronze medal for all around. The well-built Christa was a real contrast to the thin Merilyn Chapman, showing a mature beauty of form. The tiny Kelly McCoy, who is almost hipless, like many of the Russians, also had performed at her peak to come fourth. Spurred on by this, Christa was rewarded by the USGF sending her to Canada to enter the brand-new Pacific Rim Tournament, in which, for the first time, mainland China was to become a major threat.

In the Edmonton meet, Christa Canary performed very well indeed and placed second after top scorer, Wen-Chu Ma of China. Canada and Australia were the other countries entered.

Christa also scored an upset win in France, when she entered the Antibes Tournament in 1978.

Many of the top-ranked young gymnasts, such as Tatiana Arshannikova of the USSR, were on hand. This time, however, the Americans were seen as gymnasts to watch, following their great success in Moscow and Riga. The attractive girl from Illinois proved soon enough that people were right. She was only one of a small number who performed the difficult double back somersault in her floor routine. Christa's tumbling is strong and high and her vaulting great, as her 9.75 score showed. The Chinese were also in this meet and did very well. But, it was Christa's great beam routine, which brought her the 9.80 that won the day for the American girl. She was the winner of the all around title over the Russian Arshannikova, who was assumed earlier to be a sure thing for the title. Since she had also to defeat Steffi Kraker of East Germany, this was seen a great victory indeed for the USA.

In Orleans, site of the Orleans International meet, excitement was high. Here again it was to be a fight between the Americans and the thirteen-year-old Arshannikova. Christa lost out this time to Tatania, but still came in second, with Sharon Shapiro of the US in third place. Again, Christa's high 9.75 score on bars proved a winner. It was another great international competition for the United States, and for Christa Canary.

Just to prove that the world's medals did not lie in the hands of just a few girls, Marcia Frederick carried on in the same winning ways. Marcia made history in the United States, in 1978, by getting a perfect 10.00 score on the uneven bars event in the Championships of the USA. With her long slim legs in perfect time, Marcia swung her best routine for that score to give her a place in history. Only a year earlier Marcia had left Massachusetts to join

Marcia Frederick *(Rick Kenney)*

the club of Don Peters and Muriel Grossfeld. In all around, she came in fifth in this national meet.

Born in January, 1963, Marcia is another who was a slow mover until 1978. The five feet one 93-pounder was nine years old when she was under Leo Leger in the Pioneer Gym Club in Massachusetts. When she went to Houston to compete in Class 1 in the Houston Junior Nationals, she placed only ninth all around. She was able to score around the 9.00 mark in 1976 when she was getting ready for the USGF Junior Olympics. But then bad luck hit her and she broke her nose. When she was able to compete again, she had missed a lot of meets, of course. By 1977, her parents knew that, if their daughter was going to remain in gymnastics, she needed the best of coaching to improve. This was when they thought of sending her down to Muriel Grossfeld's famous club in Connecticut. This was the right move, as was soon seen.

Don Peters, Marcia's co-coach in Connecticut, was with her when the US went to the Golden Sands Invitational in Bulgaria. Don said that her jazzy version of the all-time favorite piece of music, "In the Mood," was a big hit with the crowd. Her vaulting was the best in the meet and brought her a medal. As expected, she won easily on the bars, with a 9.55. In the balance beam event, Marcia was once again the very best there with her 9.25 score. In the all around results, Marcia had a clear win over Natalia Karamouchka of the Soviet Union, to take the gold medal. In the finals, Marcia again scored the highest, with a 9.80, to win the gold medal for uneven bars. Not content with the all around title, Marcia also won the vault!

What a great competition this had to have been for a girl with really no international experience at all. And, to make her win seem all the greater, was the fact that when she got her 10.00 for her bars routine in the Championships of the USA, she had only barely recovered from a leg injury. Her mother has been wary of having her perform because the cast had come off her leg just two and a half weeks earlier. That she not only took part but got a 10.00 score, does somehow show what a fine competitor she is, and how very brave.

Then, at the 1978 Strasbourg world championships, Marcia took the first gold medal ever won by an American in this annual event with her 9.95 performance on the parallel bars.

Marcia has thoughts about being an animal doctor in the future, or at least wants to work with animals in some way. She dearly loves horses and dogs. The brown-eyed, brown-haired Marcia likes to water-ski also. Asked about favorite events, she will say bars and beam. Her mother says she loved going abroad and, of course, winning medals at the same time.

Rhonda Schwandt, who is four feet eleven inches and weighs 95 pounds, is coached by Steve Gerlach at Jetes. Rhonda won the Kips Invitational meet in the USA in 1978. She trains three and a half hours each evening, spending more time on beam than other events, but does work hard at everything until her coach tells her to stop. She thrives on having a crowd watch her, something which puts some gymnasts off. She is said to do even better under pressure, and this may be why she did so well in Europe.

Merilyn Chapman had little trouble defeating the entire team of Czech juniors when they came to the United States in 1978. Teammates Linda Kardos, Kelly McCoy and tiny Jackie Cassello took the first three places after Merilyn. The final score was 184.75 to 181.96 for the Czechs. What a great night for the American youngsters!

Christa Canary is another who loves international meets. She is captain of her gym team and works hard at making it a good team. She is the middle of three sisters. Christa has been lucky in that she has only been injured with one pulled muscle and two bruises in her career. She is a sturdy girl! She has recently started to drive and likes it. She is also fond of music, movies and swimming and is said to be a girl who feels strongly about fair play and justice for all. All in all, Christa is a great asset to her country.

From the thirteen-year-old Jackie Cassello, who is at the Connecticut Gymnastics Club along with Marcia Frederick, to Kari Lewis, Kelly McCoy, Pam Lee, Sandy Wirth and others too many to mention, the United States has a rosy future. One eleven-year-old has them all agog in Oregon right now. Her name is Tracee Talavera of the National Academy of Artistic Gymnastics. Tracee is still a skinny, mop-haired little kid, but is a great talent! Among things this unusual little girl has done, was to win the 1978 Emerald Empire Cup, beating out the medal-winning Karen Kelsall, Donna Turnbow and others. Her awesome bars routine brought the little girl a 9.55 score and she made a 9.50 on beam.

During 1978, Tracee has won the all around title in the Japanese-USA competition; the Region II all around title; the Oregon Class 1 state meet; the West Coast Junior National Championship title; and the meet known as the Rose Cup. All this, as well as the Emerald Cup! This eleven-year-old child from Oregon is a dynamic young lady, with a

Tracee Talevera   *(Michael Drousche)*

heady future. But the ultimate in short gymnasts can be claimed by Tracee. They thought Maria Filatova was small? Well, Tracee is all of four feet 4 inches tall and a hefty 62 pounds! She has yet to compete in national meets, however, and that will be the final test.

The US girls are very much up to the standard of the young Romanians, young Czechs and young Hungarians and better than most. Unless something unforeseen takes place, it seems quite likely that, by 1980, the United States of America will be ranked among the top three countries in the world, and the battle for the Olympic title could very well be between an American and a Russian.

It looks like a glorious and exciting time ahead for gymnastics in the United States, whose young boys and girls show the promise of the future. For them, and through them, will come the gold medals and the world titles. And they have achieved the perfect scores already. The only way they can go now is *up!*

Chapter 9

Hungary

For years, Hungarian women have competed in international meets but never seem to have come up with a world champion. The fine boyish gymnast, Marta Egervari, and the slender Margit Toth have been the prime women for Hungary. Then, in this last year or so, they have come up with the very pretty Eva Kanyo and Zsuzsa Kalmar. Eva Ovari is the third big name for the Hungarian team. Eva Kanyo draws the most attention. She is tallish, with a small waist and long, well-shaped legs. Although not the current style, her hair is very long and curly and she has to tie it in the back with a bow.

Eva Ovari was born in April, 1962, and has done well for herself on the world scene. When she was only 14, she came in second in the big Budapest Tournament, beaten only by Egervari. She lost to Margit Toth twice that same year but, when she performed against Romania, was able to come in second all around.

In the Grand Prix de Paris in 1977, Eva was at her peak on balance beam and was able to walk off with the bronze medal. She ended up in a fourth all around tie, a good placing for Ovari. She did not do as well in the European Championships, where, of course, more well-known gymnasts take part. In that, she was in an eleventh-place tie. However, in an international meet which pitted five countries against each other that year, Eva was again able to follow right on the heels of the older Egervari.

During the year 1977, a new name appeared in Hungarian gymnastics. It was that of a very young person, but one with a lot of talent. This was Erika Csanyi, a great little eleven-year-old. The surprising little girl not only was able to win a meet against Britain, but her scores were out of this world! They were 9.15, 9.70, 9.40 and 9.50! Erika was off and running again in a meet in Duisburg in Germany. This time her scores were better! She was able to get 9.45, 9.45, 9.40 and 9.40—a superb balance in events. The lovely Eva Kanyo had to be content with second place in this meet.

Then the Hungarians thought that Erika needed to go abroad. So they sent her to Japan to take part

Erika Csanyi *(E. Langsley)*

Eva Kanyo   (© *Volker Hischen*)

in the Japanese Junior Invitational. Wow! On floor exercise, this super teenager almost stole the show from the Russian gymnast, Agapova. She tied her in scoring with a 9.70, and only a 9.75 by Galina Ionas of the USSR took the medal from her. Her score of 38.45 gave her a fourth all around finish. In another meet in Japan, Erika won the bars title, ending with the famous Comaneci dismount. Erika has been out of the picture during 1978, possibly because of an injury as well as her age, which stops her from taking part in many international meets.

Eva Kanyo came in third in the 1977 Hungarian National Championships. To everyone's surprise, a junior, Judit Mueller, was able to come in second after Egervari. Eva won the balance beam title, one of her best events. Judit, as they say, turned the tables in England when she won the balance beam event there. The meet was the one backed by the Coca-Cola company, called the British Invitational. Judit came in second all around, as well as on bars. Her bars routine was well liked by the audience, as well as by gymnastic experts. Eva was fourth all around in this English competition.

By far Judit's best night was that at the World Cup in Spain, when she was feeling in great form. She knew she would have to take on all of the world's best; she did try hard and was able to come up with an eighth-place tie. She came close in several other events in the individuals, but did not win medals.

Thirteen-year-old Erika Flander, another really little girl, tries very hard to handle the classical routines. By classical I mean those much the same as performed by Tourischeva and Kim, to well-known pieces of music. Erika is not really ready for international meets, as she had trouble even with a junior meet in which her country met Poland. In that, she finished last of twelve girls. In a meet in England, she was able to get 71.30 points in her combined totals, which is a bit better.

Eva Kanyo must have been upset over being beaten by the "infant" Pexova back in the spring of 1977. The meet was between the Czechs and Hungarians and the ten-year-old Pexova won it very easily. True, Egervari, Ovari and Toth were not competing, and I am sure they would have left little Pexova way behind. Kanyo's scores of 37.70 showed that she did do very well, however. The fifteen-year-old Kanyo had not, at that time, much experience in competition with other countries.

Eva made her name in competition against Great Britain in 1978. For the first time, she was at her very best in three of the events, and just a bit below on vault. In this meet, Kanyo was able to defeat Marta Egervari, the Olympic competitor, on every event but vault. Eva was able to do two very good aerials—these are the high somersaults on the beam without touching the beam at all with the hands. She did two of these forward. She makes very sound use of ballet moves in her gymnastics and people point to the way she uses her long fingers and hands in routines. With her long slender legs, she is able to make most routines appear very graceful. Beam is by far one of her best events.

When Eva Kanyo came to New York for the American Cup, there were many more famous people there than her. In fact, Eva was quite unknown. The Soviet's Natasha Tereschenko was the other competitor who was not as well known as her countrywomen. In the preliminary round, which is the opening round of a two-day meet, followed the next day by the finals, Eva finished up in fifth place with 37.25. She was again able to perform very well on beam but fell, thus losing valuable points. This happens too often with the greatest performers. They fix their attention so much upon doing the hard tricks and the aerials and then they blow it on a dismount. Often the easier things are ignored and this is where they slip up.

Eva went into the finals with seven other girls and ended in seventh place, just ahead of Gheorghiu of Romania, who also had been leading the Hungarian in the first round. Gabi was not able to cope under the extra pressure of the last day. But the people watching liked the long-legged girl from Hungary, admiring her poise and grace. With her long bobbing hair, and her sweet, very lovely face, whole families liked to watch her perform. Beauty is something few people can resist.

In another meet against Switzerland, Eva was once again off form and finished fourth, with a poor 74.75. She was below normal against the East Germans with a 75.00 score and she was again beaten by Kalmar, yet, in the Hungarian Championships, she was able to come in third, behind Ovari! Eva Kanyo seems to be one of those girls who are not able to remain at one level from meet to meet.

Zsuzsa Kalmar is another young gymnast who is being seen more often. She has not really done anything out of the ordinary, but she is able to hold her own in some meets. Zsuzsa finished behind Judit Mueller in the International Tournament in Orleans in 1978. Her 36.50 was nothing special. In the meet in which her team met the British in England, she pleased the fans with her routines. She does not have the class that Kanyo has, but is a hard worker who is not afraid to try different moves. She came

Zsuzsa Kalmar   *(© Alan E. Burrows)*

in third in the United Kingdom, behind Egervari.

In the Hungarian Invitational in 1978, which drew gymnasts from at least eight countries, Zsuzsa placed first all around, her first really big win. Her combined score of 37.15 and 37.10 was not perhaps very high, but, then, none of the scoring was high. It was seen in vaulting that the Hungarian coaches placed the board much further back than Americans do. For Kalmar, it was put back to around seven feet. Zsuzsa won the floor exercise as well as the uneven bars title. There was some feeling among the watchers that she was overscored and, in view of her past performances, this is very possible.

Kalmar journeyed to Riga for their big meet and was able to come in only sixth, tied with Linda Kardos. She did not place in any of the single events and neither did Eva Kanyo, whose best was a sixth in floor.

It is really very odd that the best Romanian girls these past few years have been Magyars, those with Hungarian backgrounds. Yet the Hungarian girls do not seem to be able to really hang in there long enough to pick up medals outside their own country. Judit Mueller and Erika Csanyi appear to be two who very well may take the crown away from the veteran Marta Egervari. Right now, they need a bit more talent. When that comes, they will once again be world contenders.

Chapter 10

Canada

As she completed her final tumbling run, the spectators cheered. A Canadian girl was going to win! This was very unusual. Many times before, when they had had big meets in Canada, no one had even expected such a thing. This competition was called the Coca-Cola Invitational. The word "invitational" in meets means that gymnasts from certain countries have been invited to take part.

In Canada, gymnasts from Romania, the German Democratic Republic, the Federal Republic of Germany (West Germany), France, the United States, the Soviet Union and Japan gathered at this Ontario Cup competition. While Romania did not have her best, the best from the German Democratic Republic (East Germany) was there in the form of Silvia Hindorff. So when little Karen Kelsall, all of fourteen years old, was given a score of 9.60 for her uneven bars routine, her countrymen went wild!

All Karen's scores were over 9.50, very good indeed. The director of Sports Ontario said this about Karen that night: "Well coached, and last up, she decided to do a technically correct routine. . .This was Karen Kelsall's night and for Dick and Linda Mulvihill, a tribute to their coaching abilities.'' In the meet held in Alberta that week, also run by Coca-Cola, Karen finished first in floor exercise and tied with teammate Elfi Schlegel in vault.

How did Karen manage to get this far when so many other Canadians have not? Well, let us look at the young Karen Kelsall. Karen was born on December 11, 1962. The Kelsalls moved to California when their child was little, and it was in Clovis, California, that Karen first went to school. When she was three years old, her mother took her for ballet and dance lessons. The little girl soon learned. Her father had taken gymnastics in high school. Mrs. Kelsall had been a student of dance for seventeen years, later becoming an instructor.

When she was eight, Karen joined the Fresno Ballet Society. She had a lot of agility and loved to dance, so she was soon going to the Fresno Gymnastics Club three nights a week. When she was nine years old she joined the competitive program. This is where girls compete against each other for scores, in meets.

By 1972, Karen had gone into state competition. She won her first medal—gold—that year. This was for her winning floor exercise. Not long after this her family had to move back to Canada to live. She had been classed as Class II in the United States when she had gone home, but this was a problem. Canada does not have the same system for putting its girls in classifications. There they have names, such as Midget, Argo, Tyro and Novice. In the United States it would be Class 1, 2 and 3, and so on.

When Karen was ten she was ranked as a novice in the age group known as Argo. However, a man called John Hemingway thought she was better

Karen Kelsall   *(John Bovard)*

than most and he said he wanted to train her as a
junior, a higher grading. After a year with Hemingway, Karen moved to the Flicka Club in Van-
couver under head coach Gladys Hartley. Mrs.
Hartley's daughter had been on the 1968 Olympic
team, so having her in the club was a great help to
the young girls. Karen spent four hours training at
this time, six days a week. This is an awful lot for
anyone, and more so if you are only eleven.

About this time Karen was to meet another well-
known Canadian gymnast called Patti Rope. Patti
was working out of the National Academy of Artistic Gymnastics in Oregon, in the United States.
Training there was very hard, and it was said to be
a very fine gymnastic center. This made Karen
think. She talked to her parents and they, too, gave
it much thought. She would have to live 450 miles
from her home and that was a long way. But she
was good in the sport and, if she was to get even
better, would this not be the best way? So it was
decided. Karen was to go to Oregon.

When she was there, Karen was well looked after
by the family of Mulvihills, including Dick's mother. Although she lived in a private house, it was
called a "dormitory." The girls have bedrooms
which they share with one other girl. Karen was
very happy there, although she did miss her mother
and father. But here it was that Karen began to
become an international star under the guidance of
Dick and Linda Mulvihill.

Karen had tried out for the Canadian team back
in 1975 but had not made it. She was going to try
again, however. Now that she was with the
Mulvihills, she felt sure she would improve. Karen
did. She entered the third Olympic trials in Canada
in early 1976 where her score was good enough for

a place on the national championship team. She entered this championship meet and won the junior women title. By now it was understood that Karen would make the Canadian Olympic team.

She did not cause any great alarm to the foreign gymnasts who were there. This was because they did not think she could win. Karen did not win any medals, but she did well to finish in twenty-seventh place out of so many competitors from all over the world. Her score of 18.75 for floor exercise was one which brought cheers from the audience. She had such a nice way of doing the tricks, always happy-looking, and always so pretty, too.

In the Milk Meet in Canada that year of 1976, Karen finished second all around, although she did not do as well when she went to Japan, placing tenth in a meet there. At the American Cup in New York, Karen did not have to face the world's best girls. Many of the East Europeans did not come, and it was not a surprise that the American girls won. Karen took third place, but she did some new elements or moves and this made the crowd notice her.

By 1977, after winning the Coca-Cola meets we talked about before, Karen was classed as Canada's number one gymnast. She was only five feet and around 90 pounds but with a lot of energy and willingness to try everything. Karen has had one or two spills when performing and hurt herself. This has kept her from winning some events. When a team from Bulgaria came, in 1978, Karen placed third all around. The visiting team coach said he was amazed at the way the Canadian girls had learned and now were able to beat Europeans. Karen was very happy to hear this, of course. Her teammates, Elfi Schlegel and Monica Goermann, did very well also.

By now, Karen has lots of medals from all the many meets she has taken part in over the years. But she is not cocky about it. She is modest and feels she has had a lot of help in getting to where she has. She has had a move named after her—the Kelsall Stretch. Not even some of the young Romanian or Russian girls have had this happen!

When Karen won the 1977 Senior Women's Nationals in Canada she used for music to go with her floor exercise the French-Canadian song, "Allouette," as well as the popular "I Love Paris." With her blonde hair and her slender figure, she was in perfect timing with the music. Everyone loved her routine and so did the judges. They gave her a 9.55 score to win the event.

Although she is so very active outside, Karen Kelsall likes to do needlepoint and crochet. This takes a lot of patience. She does play tennis and likes to swim and play with her niece. Imagine, a niece, when the auntie is only fifteen years old! She does love small children and she teaches little Traci to do gymnastics.

Another bouncy little girl is Elfi Schlegel of the Xoces-Eagles Club in Toronto. Elfi was born May 17, 1964, and is in the eighth grade. On seeing her, some people have laughed, "Why, she's no bigger than a peanut!" True, Elfi is very small. But it's what she does that counts. She is already carded B in Canada, up from her 1977 C rating. In Japan's Chunichi Cup, she was a great favorite. She came in at seventh all around, a good place for someone with so little international experience. In the *Moscow News* meet in the Soviet Union, that big annual event, Elfi's scores were ranked tenth. Because there is only one place for each girl entered, they list by number of girls. This means that when three girls tied for eighth place, the next girl is ranked eleventh, even though her score is right behind the eighth girl. Well, Elfi placed twelfth because of a tie, although her score was the tenth best.

Elfi Schlegel   *(Courtesy International Gymnast)*

When it came time for the Coca-Cola Invitational, Elfi was not at her sparkling best. She placed fifth all around in Ontario. Then came the Alberta meet, and things got better. Here she won the uneven bar event over famous people like Grigoras of Romania and Glutschenko of the Soviet Union. She tied Karen Kelsall in both floor exercise and in the vault, a great win for this dainty little blonde girl with the ponytail.

In the United States in 1977, Elfi entered the Emerald Cup. In this she placed third all around. It seemed she was always doing better each time she went into another meet.

When the Bulgarian team came in 1978, Elfi was waiting. This was to be her big chance and she did not miss it. She may have been only four feet seven inches tall, but she had a big heart. She did not do as well in Manitoba, where her all around was 74.95, but it was good enough to place her second all around behind Karen. Then came her day. Ontario was ready. Elfi was ready. She looked at the crowd, she looked at the vault, the beam, the bars. This was to be her challenge. Off she went! Light as a feather, she hurtled through the routines. When it was all over that night, Elfi was the toast of Toronto. She had won the uneven bar title with a high 9.75, her 70 pounds slicing the air with daring speed. She easily won the floor exercise, with her 9.70 score. Balance beam wasn't so easy. She settled for a tie here. But her vault brought her a 9.70, which was not enough to win, but did bring her the all around title. To win the title, plus two of the events with ease and one shared, had to have been a very happy event for this little Ontario gymnast. "I really felt good tonight," she said, "I was working some new moves into my routine, so I guess I was lucky I didn't make any bad mistakes."

Well, she did not make many later that May either. This was the forty-second Canadian National Championships. Karen Kelsall, Sherry Hawco, Monica Goermann—all were there to show what they could do. But, in the end, it was that elf from the club with the funny name who won the senior women's title. Yes, Elfi Schlegel put together a total of 75.15 points to win over second place Karen Kelsall. She was able to perform a really great floor routine and audience and judges thought she deserved the 9.75 score. Elfie always uses music to suit her tiny frame. Music like that from *H.M.S. Pinafore* and sailors' hornpipes. Every gymnast has to use music which goes with her body style. Elfi uses some that seems right for her small person. Her coaches, Mary Lea and Geoff Palmer, know how wrong music can hurt a gymnast.

Elfi has a six-year-old sister taking gymnastics, so it is possible the name will be around for a long time to come! Elfi gets lots of fan mail from all over, mostly from Japan. Like most gymnasts, she only goes to school mornings so she can have the afternoons to train. When she is not at school, she likes to ride bikes, loves to travel, and enjoys shopping. Her week is very, very full, but this little girl with the perky face uses every minute to make things count.

Another girl, Monica Goermann, is also on the national team. She, too, has a European background, and this has helped her gymnastics. Born in Winnipeg, September 1, 1964, she attends high school in the eighth grade. Monica is a member of the Winnipeg Gymnastics Center, the team known as the Winnettes. She is coached by her mother and

Monica Goermann   *(Courtesy Monica Goermann)*

father, as well as by Rick Shore.

Monica trains about twenty-five hours a week and this, as you will see, has paid off. She takes three hours a week of ballet with the Royal Winnipeg Ballet company, which is very useful to any gymnast. Oddly enough, Nadia Comaneci did not take ballet when she was younger and some think she does not have the grace of those who did.

Monica placed third in the annual selection meet when she was only twelve. First and second were Karen and Elfi, of course. With long sturdy legs and a slender body, she has shown that she has lots of talent. Over in Russia, in 1977's *Moscow News* meet, she came in thirteenth—very good indeed for the number of girls in it and in view of Monica's age of just twelve. In the Canadian Junior Championships that same year, she came in second all around, winning titles on vault and on floor. She was also second on bars. Already provincial champion of Manitoba, Monica, by now, was also looking for a European title. She didn't win it but she did place ninth all around out of twenty-five girls entered. Most of the others were girls who had been in many more international meets, too. Monica did win a medal, a bronze, for her floor exercise, and she barely missed one for beam, placing fourth. Her teammate, Sherry Hawco, another exciting fourteen-year-old, was performing in Riga. She did not win, but she also came in ninth.

Happy with her medal, Monica was bound to do greater things and, when she went to London for the British Champions All, she proved herself. She tied for first in floor exercise and won a gold medal. Because ten countries sent girls, her sixth place finish was very good. After all, she was only thirteen years old!

Back home in Canada, Monica was to show her thrilled family that they had a famous name in their house now. She went out to perform against the Bulgarians. This was in 1978 and, by now, Monica had learned a lot more. Her parents had been born in Germany and loved to see their daughter doing so well in this sport they both loved. In Winnipeg that night, against the Bulgarian team, Monica's star had never shone brighter. Monica Goermann won the all around title over Kelsall, Schlegel and the Bulgarian girls. She had been in second place after the compulsories, but was able to make up enough points in the optionals to win. Like the other girls, she wants to be in the 1980 Olympics.

All the Canadian girls are pretty to look at and have fresh cheerful faces. They perform as though they really enjoy what they are doing. Elfi and Karen have the same happy look. To them just to be a part of gymnastics is fun. But to win medals as well—that is the icing on top of the cake!

Canada has shown it has talented young girls, with lots of courage who are lots of fun to watch. The number of people in their country is small, in view of the size of their land. This means they do not have as many people to choose from as some of the countries with more people. But if they have even a few, such as Monica, Elfi and Karen, they have a great future. Other young girls, like Carmen Alie and Sherry Hawco are being sent to foreign meets. Maybe they, too, will bring back medals one day and make this big country proud of the young gymnasts who live in it.

Chapter 11

Poland

Dare I say that there might be another Nadia in a little-known gymnastic country—Poland? The name of this sprite, with a little-boy haircut and slightly pointed ears, is Anita Jokiel. Sounds like an elf? Yes, and she looks a bit like one too! She's a tiny little girl, all of four feet four inches in height, with a sweet smile and light blue eyes.

Anita was born early December in 1966. At the age of 11, she has already taken part in international meets and has looked terrific. Because of her age she cannot yet take part in the major competitions. With her little bit of weight, 56 pounds, she is able to do very rapid tumbling. She is light enough to propel herself off the floor with quick handsprings. In fact, she is able to use her body in a way only mature girls usually do.

Poland has long had an active team of male gymnasts, but has not done well with its women. None were of Olympic calibre in 1976. Only the veteran Lucia Matraszek, born in 1954, has been able to compete with any kind of high standard over the past few years. The Poles are very aware of this shortcoming and are trying very hard to come up with some good girls in the near future. They feel that they have two we should make a note of, in addition to their delightful little Anita.

Anita Jokiel
(Courtesy Polish Gymnastic Federation)

Elzbieta Szewczak and Wieslawa Zelaskowska
(Courtesy Polish Gymnastic Federation)

Elzbieta Szewczak, who was born on September 10th, 1965, is a good uneven bar worker. She is a member of the club called OKS "Stomil" in the town of Olsztyn. Elzbieta is a pupil at a grade school, as are the other two girls. She was able to perform really well in the big *Moscow News* meet in April, 1978. In this she tied for seventeenth place out of 46 girls. Along with her in that score came Tatiana Lickova of Czechoslovakia and Nabuko Kasai of Japan. Sometimes we read that a girl finished in seventeenth place and we think that this does not seem very good. But, when we also know that 46 girls took part, this means that she was better than 29 others!

The names of these girls are not said the way they look. The letter "W" is said like a "V," which brings me to Wieslawa Zelaskowska. She was born in October, 1964, and you would say her name *Veeslava Zhellaskovskah!* Wieslawa is four feet eight inches tall and weighs 79 pounds. She, too, is a member of the OKS "Stomil" club in Olsztyn, where she is trained by Zbigniew and Krystyna Zolnierowicz. (Elzbieta has the same couple coaching her, by the way.) Wieslawa was a finalist in the high bar competition, where she came in seventh, in the Friendship Cup meet. She has been in gymnastics since she was nine and is now a member of the national team.

Elzbieta, who is now thirteen years old and is four feet nine inches tall, is 79 pounds in weight. She, like her teammate Wieslawa, likes to wear a puffy bow in her long ponytailed hair. Where Wieslawa is darker of hair and eyes, Elzbieta has fair hair and light eyes. For her height, Wieslawa is fairly heavy with strong sturdy legs.

In the 1977 meet in Antibes, France, Zelaskowska was able to come in at tenth all around. Her score was 36.70, which was really great for a girl only twelve years old. This shows that she has learned a lot in her few years within the sport. Elzbieta is another good uneven bars gymnast. She came in sixth in the *Moscow News* meet held on March 29th, 1978, in this event. She did not do as well in the combined scoring later, however. This is a very big, exciting competition for a young girl, and it does take its toll in making her nervous and able to make mistakes.

Anita Jokiel's trainers, as they call coaches in Europe, are her parents. She has been in gymnastics only since 1974, when she was eight. Although she had only these few years of training, she was able to enter the International Championships in the German Democratic Republic in the spring of 1978. This meet was for gymnasts under the age of fourteen. Anita was then twelve years old. She not only competed against girls older than she, but she won the competition!

Anita was sent to the new Coca-Cola Invitational in England in December of 1977. This perhaps was expecting too much from a very young girl. Remember, she had her eleventh birthday just four days before the meet! And this was a very hectic two-day competition for an eleven-year-old child. Among the 34 gymnasts on hand, the little Polish girls did quite well. Wieslawa came in tenth all around; Elzbieta, thirteenth; and Anita—the baby—finished in fifteenth place. Anita did a great job with her floor routine, amid thunderous applause. She did not do well in her uneven bars, however, and had a terrible fall from the top bar. She ended up in tears, which made the audience feel very sorry for her. She soon smiled through them and her perky little face lit up once again. She really has an endearing face and she certainly does try those hard tricks.

In a meet against Hungary in 1977, Wieslawa was able to place second all around and Anita fifth all around. In the major meet in Czechoslovakia, the Kosice Tournament, some 36 girls took part. In this, Wieslawa was in eighteenth place at the end, with only good floor and balance beam scores. This was held in April, 1978, and there were many of the top young Russian and Czech girls taking part, so competition was probably harder.

Because of their age, and the hope that they will continue to get better, we can see a great future for the young Polish team. That they are able to handle international competitions at eleven years old is quite unusual. Of course, we knew that this was possible because Nadia started to become well-known at this age. It may be that Poland, one of these days, will echo to the sounds of "Come on, Anita!" And it could be that we will hear little girls say, "Gee, I wish I was as good as Anita Jokiel."

Chapter 12

Bulgaria

Bulgaria had been fairly quiet since the Olympics, until 1978, when they started to tour more. They, too, had used their older women in 1976 and seemed not to have too many young ones coming up, something several countries have found to be true. Their top gymnasts, such as Nadia Chatarova and Maria Kirtcheva who were members of the Bulgarian Olympic team, are still competing, but other names are cropping up.

Among the newcomers are Antoanet Rahneva, who is now fourteen years old. Another is Krassimira Toneva, who has been injured but seems to have recovered. Krassimira is thirteen years old and is said to be a very talented young girl. She is able to get scores in the low nines in all her events, but is not always very even with them. Sometimes she does well, sometimes not. Krassimira Verbanova was the best Bulgarian, in fifth place. Miss Toneva failed and was injured in this meet, held in mid-1978.

Toneva is a good dancer and her floor routine was one of the best seen at the Canada-Bulgaria meet in 1978. She placed second in this event, with teammate Chatarova. Verbanova did well in bars and vault. In the all around in Ontario, Dilana

Glutscheva had a high finish, winning the third-place bronze medal. Verbanova came in tenth and Toneva fourteenth. Dilana came in twelfth in the Riga Cup competition in 1978 but her scores were fairly low.

In Varna in 1977, Rahneva reappeared. She came in first out of 36 girls entered in this Varna International. She beat out the older Chatarova with a score of 36.50. Svetla Krasteva also has been seen more and more in major meets. She tied for seventh in balance beam in the Hungarian Invitational in 1978. Glutscheva had one of her better meets at the *Moscow News,* where she came in ninth all around. In the finals, her floor exercise gave her a sixth-place finish. She was twelfth all around in the Riga Cup.

Maja Isakova, Penka Zelaskova, Rumjana Miluseva and Galina Marinova are all girls who enter meets in Europe. So far none of these young Bulgarians have been able to make a name for themselves in any competition. Sometimes they have entered as many as six girls in one meet—surely meaning that they do have plenty of gymnasts available. The team that toured Canada in 1978 had eight girls on it! This means that they have the interest in the sport, but not yet the ability.

There is no one likely to challenge Nadia or Natalia for some years I think. The Bulgarians are nice, attractive girls, and seem to enjoy their performances as much as the audience does. In the Golden Sands Invitational, Krassimira Verbanova put a spark of hope in Bulgarian hearts when she happily finished in sixth all around—a high finish for a Bulgarian. Maybe this shows the way for the other girls to follow.

Chapter 13

Great Britain

The sturdy, fair-haired girl was performing her final vault. Over she went! What a fine vault that was. Great height and a solid landing. The crowd cheered lustily. They were biased, of course. The competition was Champions All and the gymnast was their own girl from Huddersfield, Karen Robb.

Karen is from the county known as Yorkshire, in England. England is one of four ancient countries which made up the United Kingdom or Great Britain. All the girls are British, but they are either English, if they come from England, Welsh if they come from Wales, Scottish if they come from Scotland and Irish or Ulsterwomen, if they come from Northern Ireland or Ulster. They are all part of Great Britain's team and compete under that name.

Karen came in third in Champions All, tying with the girl from the German Democratic Republic, Silvia Hindorff. Karen does not do too well in her beam routines and this loses her points. She is a great tumbler and vaulter. Denise Jones, also from Huddersfield, is thought to be one of the best. Denise is fifteen years old, and so one of the older gymnasts in this book, most of which is devoted to the younger or lesser-known girls. Denise won the highly prized Russian Scholarship in 1977. This special competition is for gymnasts from thirteen to fifteen. The winner spends a month in Moscow training with Russian coaches. In 1976, Karen Robb came in second in this. That same year, Great Britain won the World Schools Championships in France, with Karen Robb placing third in the individual awards.

The British girls have all been heavier than other national gymnasts. They have been heavy of thigh and body, unlike the skinny Romanians and Russians. This has hurt their performances in events like beam and uneven bars.

The clubs and schools in Britain help their gymnasts train and travel. The England Schools Gymnastics Association sends out books on gymnastics. These books have drawings and describe each move under the drawing. They also show the right and wrong ways that routines are done.

In the National Development Plan, gymnasts are graded and, while the schools are the base of gymnastics in Britain, the government provides many centers for competition.

Another group which has helped with gymnastics in England has been the newspapers. The world-famous *Sunday Times* is a sponsor and so is the *Daily Mirror*. A sponsor is a group or person who gives money or aid to help put on a competition. The Champions All meet is run by the *Daily Mirror,* and so is the national meet called the Champions Cup. Many reporters have also written books about well-known gymnasts, and some newspapers make posters of gymnasts. They are all part of the gymnastics scene. The *Sunday Times* has sponsored national schools championships as well as the magazine, *The Junior Gymnast*. The *Daily Mirror* sponsors the visiting Soviet teams each year, along with the gymnastics federation, which is known as the British Amateur Gymnastics Association or BAGA.

Other sponsors include the Coca-Cola Company, Lilia-White Company and Outline Company. Lilia-White makes women's medical items, and the Lilia-White National Championships have proven very popular. These companies are of great value in any country where the state does not provide free programs. It would be very hard indeed to put on competitions without their help. The Lilia-White Company also has a scholarship which started in 1976. They pick some twenty girls between the ages of twelve and sixteen and send them to a training center for one week each year. The girls get personal coaching in this program, which is of great help to all the gymnasts.

The national squad of Britain is made up this way: It is divided into age groups. One would be from age thirteen to age fifteen, with about sixteen gymnasts. Then there are the eleven to thirteen year olds, also with about sixteen gymnasts. The squad is broken down into North and South for part of its training. Some ten-year-olds are part of this squad also. The areas of the country in which girls take part are known as regions. When there is a meet held in a region, it is called a regional. About forty gymnasts are working in each of the regional squads. The over-fifteen age group has 20 gymnasts who train in an A and B Squad.

A panel of people work with the national squad, planning its training times and floor exercise music, and helping as much as it can. They are also working on a four-year program for elite gymnasts and another for the lower level of gymnast. They feel they have done much already, as proved by the way Britain keeps winning the World Schools Championships. It is only at the higher levels that the British teams have not done well, and this is where the BAGA and people working inside the sport know they must get better. The British federation has been active for ninety years and admits that gymnastics is growing in leaps and bounds every year. This means they must work much harder if they want to make some international champions.

During the past seven years alone, over two million badges have been awarded to gymnasts taking part in the *Sunday Times*-BAGA awards program. This is a lot when you think that this small nation has only sixty million people! The people have a lot of pride in what they do, but they are not a nationalist people in the sense that they feel they must win or they will not take part. There is no force used to make gymnasts work hard; they take part because they love to perform. Winning medals is fun for them, but they do not take losing as badly as other countries. This is good, but hurts in international competition. The will to win is what makes winners, after all.

Some of the girls who might just bring medals to Britain are those who belong to the Huddersfield Club. One young lady is already raising eyebrows and causing people to cheer. She is Kathy Williams, who was fourteen in February, 1978. Kathy only started in gymnastics when she was ten, in her home town of Manchester in the North of England. Kathy belonged to a small club, so did not have any real knowledge of national meets until she moved to the Huddersfield Club. Under coach

Kathy Williams *(© Alan E. Burrows)*

Janet Mitchell, Kathy started to make rapid progress. She got better with each performance. She is a very small, slim little black girl. Her two younger brothers and a sister are also good gymnasts.

Kathy entered the Lilia-White Competition, which is for the under 16s, in 1977. At thirteen, she did very well, but she did not win. One thing noted was her very good tumbling. She looks good in her arm movements and this makes her floor exercise nice to watch. She won the Soviet Gymnastics Scholarship (which is sponsored by the *Daily Mirror* and the British Gymnastics Association) during 1978, beating out Jackie Bevan who was a close second.

Nicola Meek   *(Courtesy Nicola Meek)*

In the British women's team championships in 1978, twenty-seven clubs entered the first round. Because of the fine work of Denise Jones and Kathy Williams, the Huddersfield Club won the title for juniors. One tiny girl to catch the eye was with the Loughton Club. Her name is Nicola Meek and she is only eleven years old. At her age, she has limited experience, of course. Still, she was seen to land her Tsukahara vault well and she does a nice floor exercise. Nicola started gymnastics under Linda Taylor at East Herts College. She has moved to work now under Colin and Christine Still at Loughton Hall Club. In 1977, Nicola became the eighth grade champion. This was very good for Nicola and made her very happy. Then, in 1978, Nicola pleased her coaches again and became the seventh grade gymnastics champion! Kathy Williams was the Grade 5 champion.

Kathy is built almost the same as any eleven-year-old Romanian or Russian, very straight up and down, with thin legs. This gives her good repulsion on her vault. Repulsion is the word they use to talk about push off or lift off.

Nicola was chosen to be with the English Schools Gymnastic team against Scotland and Wales, as well as against the Federal Republic of Germany (West Germany). She did not win the under 13s title in the English Schools meet, but she did place third. Nicola is highly rated as a result of this. To look at, she is blonde, hair tied-up in a knot, with a short body. She seems to be a natural dancer, natural meaning that she dances with ease and good style. Nicola reminds one of the Canadian girl, Elfi Schlegel.

Amanda O'Neil is a sturdier girl. She has solid shoulders, good for uneven bars and tumbling. She

Amanda O'Neil *(Courtesy Amanda O'Neil)*

is thirteen years old and with Colin Still's Loughton Hall Club. She is a member of the national squad and has been on the England team against Scotland and Wales, and against West Germany. In the Loughton Open meet in 1977, Amanda placed fifth. In this competition, she stunned the audience by doing a back somersault on the beam, as well as some nice walkovers. She can also do a cartwheel with a full twist in her dismount. Amanda won the all around title in the under 13s EGSA Championship. Because Nicola came in third in this, we can see good work from coaches Colin and Christine Still at Loughton Hall. Amanda is doing some hard tricks already, which include a back walkover flip on beam. This shows that she is not afraid to try things and could mean a future champion for the Stills.

The difficulty side of gymnastics has been the main reason British gymnasts have not been scored higher. Difficulty is the term given to the F.I.G. rating system. Each move is given a points rating. If you do a superior move, or one that has a high number of points, then you score higher. Olga Korbut was known to be a great performer of high-difficulty routines. She would try every hard trick possible. The Romanians are able to do the same, but not the British until the last year or so.

Kathy Williams is one of the best to come along and people hope she will become a future champion. She finished fourteenth in the 1978 Junior European Championships—very good for a British girl. In the National Development Plan finals, Kathy scored over 9.00 points average for all of the events and was the only one to do so. She showed solid moves on the bars, something which frightens a lot of young gymnasts in Britain. Her work on the balance beam was as sound as that on the floor exercise and better than many of the other girls competing. Kathy is well liked by everyone who knows her and this makes the crowds like what she does also. Some girls do better when the audience gives them a lot of support. As we said earlier, Kathy won the USSR Gymnastics Scholarship. Kathy, whose full name is Kathleen, will be able to attend the Vladimir School of Gymnastics near Moscow. She makes her home in Manchester in England, where she attends the Central High School for Girls. All the previous winners have done very well for Great Britain and Kathy hopes to follow in their footsteps. One of these winners was Denise Jones.

Denise has still a way to go before she peaks or reaches her best. She came in third in the Loughton Open, which was won by teammate and top British star, Karen Robb. In the EGSA Past and Present meet, Denise tied for fourth place. Just before Christmas, 1977, Denise took part in the British individual apparatus championships. The three best British gymnasts were from the older group. Karen Leighton, Karen Robb and Susan Cheeseborough, British women's champion. Right on their tails was Denise, however. She showed some good skills in this meet, but just did not have the knowledge of competition that the other girls had.

Denise won the Grade 3 title in the National Development Plan finals. She did not do well on uneven bars that day, but she was really at her best on vault. Her vault, known as a piked Tsukahara, was said to be "out of this world." Her best performance by far came during the Champions Cup. Denise was thrilled about taking part and showing what she could do in front of the fans in the famous

Denise Jones   *(Pete Huggins)*

old building known as the Albert Hall. Although Karen Robb won the Cup, followed by Susan Cheeseborough, one writer said, "The biggest impact among the challengers was made by fifteen-year-old Denise Jones, in her first appearance in the competition." She landed her Korbut back well in her exciting balance beam routine. She vaulted well and with courage. She did have a fall on her dismount off the uneven bars and that hurt her chance to come in second. In the 1978 British Women's Team Championships, Denise Jones had the highest single score. Her score, and that of the little Manchester girl, Kathy Williams, brought the title to Huddersfield. Denise's greatest triumph in international competition came in midsummer, 1978, when she won a silver medal for both uneven bars and a very good vault in the World School Games. Only the Chinese were able to beat this pretty girl from Yorkshire. Denise even picked up a bronze medal for her exciting beam routine.

Among other young, promising gymnasts are Louise Miler, who is fourteen. Louise has had an injury which kept her out of action too long. Another, who works out under Yvonne Saunders at the Ladywell Club, is a twelve-year-old called Sally Dewhurst. She is now on the junior international squad, and is said to be a very hard-working, firm-minded young girl. She has performed the Tsukahara vault in meets and is trying out the double twist in her floor exercise routine. These gymnasts are all possible stars of the future for Great Britain.

Clubs and schools are trying to help gymnasts avoid injury as much as they can. Several of the clubs have put in filled pits, so that young gymnasts can fall without hurting themselves. It also makes a girl feel more secure if she knows that, should she fall, she will not get hurt. The Russians have these pits in most sports areas as well. Businesses continue to do more to help. Steiner's, a large hair products company, has started a new scholarship for gymnasts in Yorkshire, the county where the city of Huddersfield is. The first check was handed over to Lord Harewood, president of a group called the Yorkshire and Humberside Sports Fund for the Gifted. This money will go to help girls like Kathy, Denise and other Yorkshire gymnasts.

When you think that over seven hundred girls take part in the regional competitions, those meets held in different regions in order to find the best girls to go into the finals, it is really amazing. Some clubs have three hundred or more gymnasts. One club with 320 youngsters from age five up, has a waiting list of two hundred gymnastic hopefuls. Another twelve-year-old girl from a club in the county of Berkshire moved to Iran a couple of years ago. Last year, she was chosen to perform for the Iranian shah in front of 100,000 people, along with Iranian girl gymnasts. The famous Huddersfield Gym Club put on a terrific show for the New Year in 1977, when they had three performances, each with two hundred gymnasts! This, of course, is the way to bring the sport to those people who have never seen it.

Britain's Minister of Sport, Dennis Howell, said last year that "gymnastics is a sport which calls for great dedication and courage, and it is nice to know that our nation is producing so many children with these qualities." What a wonderful thing to say about young gymnasts! It shows again that one does not always have to win medals in competition to be highly thought of by your own country. Britain has never been a big power in international gymnastics. It is a small nation with not that many people. But, as the minister said, it is producing many young people now who have great courage and who can stick at it until they get better. And they will!

Chapter 14

The Federal Republic of Germany

It is really sad that the Federal Republic of Germany (West Germany) has been so slow at rebuilding after so many of its girls retired from competition. Andrea Bieger, Petra Kurbjuweit, Ute Maiwald and Judith Werb have been keeping the gymnastics reins for too long. Not that West Germany does not enter enough competitions—it does. It also has 180 gymnastic districts and almost three million gymnasts as members of its federation. In the children's category, which is from age four to age fourteen, there are about 790,000 girls. From age fifteen to eighteen, there are another 166,000 girls. The Youth Organization is given money to help it along by the German government, so there is no lack of funds to help sport.

Every four years, the Federal Republic holds a huge gymnastics festival at which there are often from 65,000 to 70,000 gymnasts entered. They have good programs for the gymnasts, and even have a mother and child gymnastic program, as well as he and she programs, so that the whole family is involved. Because of all this effort, is is hard to explain why they do not have world calibre gymnasts.

Ute Maiwald is still a top gymnast, at eighteen. Andrea and Martina Bieger are continuing to compete also. Andrea is now nineteen and was on the Olympic team along with Petra, who is twenty-one years old. Tamara Reiter, at seventeen, was one of the bigger stars for the West Germans. Tamara is the daughter of a wealthy businessman and can afford the time to travel to meets. Tamara came in second in the Wereld Top in The Netherlands (Holland) in 1977.

Girls who are doing well now and ones to watch are Annette Michler and Annette Toifle, who are fifteen and sixteen years old. In a round for girls to qualify for the European Championships, Annette Michler, then only thirteen, made a mess-up of her uneven bar exercise, for a low 8.50 score. Had she not done so she might very well have gone with Petra and the others to Prague. The winner of that meet was the fifteen-year-old Tamara Reiter, now sixteen.

Wiebke Hunn came into the picture around that time and was in and out of a lot of meets. Her scoring was not that good, being in the eights through the low nines. Kirstin Kleiter also made an appearance. She also scored too low to be noticed. In a meet against Hungary, Wiebke was able to come in third, after Eva Kanyo. All her scores were in the low nines. Kirsten, meanwhile, was sent in against England and here she did much better. She won the gold medal with 36.55.

Fraulein Michler tried again against the Swiss, but her scores were not worthy of note, although she placed fourth in all around. In this meet, another Annette, Toifle, came in sixth all around, but with every score out of compulsory and optionals in the eights, but for three just over 9, she would probably want to forget the whole thing. Wiebke was really out of her class in this meet, being buried

Annette Michler
(Courtesy German Federal Republic Gymnastic Federation)

Annette Toifle　*(Emil Schonhaar)*

at the bottom.

Annette Michler is a pretty girl with a short blonde bobbed haircut. She has lovely long fingers and is able to use her hands and arms to good advantage. In the qualifying meet for the World Championships in 1977, Annette was able to come in second after Ute Maiwald. Wiebke was third and Toifle was fourth. Scoring was low, however. Annette Michler was the balance beam champion in 1977. She is trained by Hanne Saamann in the Tus Hattingen Club.

Annette Toifle was the junior all around champion and she is trained by Rudi Seiter in the Sollingen Club. Oddly enough, Annette Michler, the balance beam champion, only got an 8.65 in the optional part of the qualifying rounds for the

World Championships. So, as one can see, being a champion in this sport does not always make you a winner! In the international competition in Orleans, Michler improved on her scoring quite a bit and came in ninth in good company. It is possible she could still surprise everyone.

In another qualifying round, Annette Toifle came in second with Wiebke third, before the veteran Petra. Scoring was poor overall. Baerbel Foerger was sixth in this after getting a high scored compulsory set. Fraulein Toifle might have a weight problem; she is a big heavy girl, who often wears her hair in a long ponytail.

Injuries have been one real problem with the West German girls. They have suffered from many injuries the past two years and this has greatly hurt their chances in international meets. Tamara Reiter, Petra Kurbjweit and Andrea Bieger are among the girls who have been injured.

The young gymnasts from West Germany have a long way to go. They have to work much harder to improve. With the funds they have, plus the millions of gymnasts, there is really no reason why they cannot by now have licked these girls into shape, or at least have made them worthy of competition on the world scene. They are all attractive, pleasant girls. It would be nice to see them on the winners' stands every now and then, as befitting the great country they come from. A ten-year-old, Gaby Kleist, is being groomed for future hopes. She is from Hamburg and may continue to do well. The Federal Republic certainly hopes so.

The Germans more than any other nation have been responsible for the birth and growth of gymnastics as a sport. Friedrich Jahn is called the father of gymnastics, and, in 1811, he was able to give to the public a playground with gymnastics apparatus. He had good students working with him and, before long, they came up with rough things to do their gymnastics on, calling them parallel bars, vaulting horse, balance beam, horizontal bar and a springboard. The horse was not his idea —it started back in the days of the Romans and Persians—but it was he who was able to adapt it to the use we know today. Because of this great man and the way that the German people have given so much to gymnastics, it is sad that they do not have a world champion among their young girls. Their men have always been good but their women have never quite been of the same high calibre. For Friedrich Jahn and his students of the 1800s, I am sure all of Germany would wish that a change might be brought about and they will get to see a gold medalist from the Federal Republic.

Chapter 15

Japan

For reasons based upon their way of life, women do not receive the same freedom in sports that men do in Japan. As a result there are not as many young Japanese girls as there are in most other countries taking part in the sport.

To give you some idea of the problems their federation has had, in the 1976 Olympics, their veteran was Miyuka Hironaka, then 31, while the youngest two girls were born in 1961!

Although they have several girls they are sending into the international scene, they have been doing very poorly. There is little at the current stage to suggest they will have anyone of the ability of even the younger Americans for some time to come. In the 1977 High School Championships, all the watchers were eager to see if anyone looked like another Nadia. Alas, they did not. In the meet, there were seven girls' teams, and about thirty girls competed on the balance beam. Only two of these girls were able to stay on the beam without falling off at one time or another. Vaulting would appear to be about their best event and is always a good event for the Japanese.

In the major meets in the world, only the men have held their own. No girls appeared among the top twenty in the World Cup in 1977. The

Sakiko Nozawa   *(© Alan E. Burrows)*

Satoko Okazaki *(Glenn Sundby)*

backbone of the Japanese team has been the two young Olympians, Satoko Okazaki and Sakiko Nozawa. Both were 17 years old in 1978. During 1977, Satoko did enter a lot of meets, including the two big ones in the Soviet Union. In the Moscow News meet, she was thirteenth all around. She did better in Riga, where she was able to tie the improving Emilia Eberle for tenth place.

Sakiko was sent to England for the 1977 Champions All, but she only scraped into eighth place, out of nine girls entered. In the Chunichi Cup, held in their own country, Sakiko tied for sixth place with Neacsu and Egervari. Her scoring was even, but low. In that big international, Ayako Akaba and Yuki Kawai came last. Akaba's top score was on vault, a 9.30. Ayako had been seen earlier, but made no great impact in any meet. She also entered the American Cup in New York in 1977 where she was seen to be a steady performer but needed more difficult moves before making it in the big time.

Satoko was in Canada in 1977 for the Coca-Cola Invitational. She did quite well on floor and beam, but poorly on the other two events. At an international in Budapest in Hungary, Okazaki was able to place sixth all around. Her 36.30 score shows that she was barely able to come over the 9.00 mark on each event. Back home it was a different matter for Satoko. In the NHK Cup in 1977, Japan's second-largest meet, she came in first all around. Akaba was fourth and Nozawi was fifth. Satoko's 9.70 for floor exercise was received with great applause. She has been very popular.

During the year 1978, Japan again tried to improve on the experience of its young girls. Teams were sent to the United States with this in mind. This did not offer any upsurge in their gymnastics, because Ayako Saito, the best Japanese girl, only came in sixth. Yoshiko Matsumoto came in seventh and Sakiko managed a ninth-place finish.

The Japanese held their trials for the World Games in June of 1978. Little Miss Nozawa was able to win the women's meet over Matsumoto, who is four years older. Okazaki tied for second with the older girl. The fifteen-year-old Kano was fourth. She had been an entrant in the 1978 American Cup, but did not make the finals; she placed fourteenth in the first day's meet. Akaba finished sixth in these trials. She was fifth on vault in the World University Games. She seems to get a lot of scores in the eights, which would place her out of most competition wins.

Okazaki is still the soundest performer. She was in such good form at the Montreal Olympics that it seemed certain she would become a top class world performer. She did not, for some reason. Her pretty little face, with the soft slanting eyes, and her tiny figure, made her very popular with the fans. She has such a nice way of weaving in and out of her moves, like poetry. Her arms and hands are so dainty and move so well. Although only four feet ten and one-half inches she was able then to perform a super uneven bar routine, which gave her a high score of 9.80. And this in the Olympic Games, mind you. Yet, in lesser meets since then, she has barely managed to place. Very strange indeed, and probably due to her changing from a young child into a teenager. This has been a real problem with many of the girls in competition. They do well until they are fifteen or sixteen and then they have a lot of extra weight, height and body problems to control.

Okazaki is from Tokyo and studied at

Kokugakuin High School. Akaba is at Tokai University. During the recent University Championships, Ayako was able to beat everyone by a clear margin. She won vault as well as beam and came in second in floor exercise. Because of the age of the girls who took part, we cannot consider any of them as future *young* prospects.

Sakiko Nozawa was another who seemed to have a great future. She toured the United States when it was unusual to do so, way back in 1973. Okazaki was with her. Both girls were then twelve years old, Sakiko being the younger by six months. Sakiko is also from Tokyo and was a student at Hachigaoka Junior High School. Both girls are dark-eyed, of course, with the rich black hair of their countrywomen.

Miss Kano would seem to be the only one, other than Okazaki and Nozawa, who might be able to achieve anything in the near future. Japan does have fine colleges and schools. One of these is the Nippon P.E. College, which visitors have said has the best gymnastic team in the country. Kokugukuin High is supposed to have the best of all the high school teams and this is where the well-known Okazaki learned her gymnastics to go to the Olympic Games. Right now, the Japanese would appear to have very few young women who are able to compete on the international level. This was true in the United States five years ago, so it may be that the Japanese, too, will be able to make a great comeback in the years ahead.

Chapter 16

Australia and New Zealand

Australia and New Zealand are parts of the British Commonwealth. Gymnastics there is not as big as in Europe, but is very popular in clubs and in schools. More and more young girls are taking up gymnastics in Australia. Some of the clubs now have as many as seven hundred or more children taking part in gymnastics. Gymnastics in this part of the world is split into A, B, and C grades and, for girls, under ten, under thirteen, under sixteen and open group above. There are novices, as in Canada, and various levels under which the children compete. They hold state championships for areas called Queensland, South Australia, Victoria and New South Wales, as well as Western Australia. Remember—this is a very big country indeed, with many areas in which no people live.

The area called New South Wales gave birth to the young Marina Sulichich, in a smallish mining town called Broken Hill. The people there are very fond of their gymnasts and they got together in 1976 to do something about it. Marina had won the under-fourteen championships, the Australian Silver Championships, the South Australia under-fourteen championships and the New South Wales championship title. At this time Marina was only

Kerry Bayliss   *(John C. Bovard)*

twelve years old! The people of Broken Hill raised money in order to send Marina and another gymnast on a tour of Hawaii and New Zealand. This shows how very loyal they are to the young people taking part in this sport.

In the 1977 championships, Marina paid them off. She won the national championships for women under thirteen, followed by Kerry Bailey. Keri Battersby won the title for under tens. Although so young, Marina was made a member of the Australian national team. In the groups called Gold, Silver and Bronze, Marina was the vault champion, the beam champion, the uneven bars champion and also the floor champion! Her group was at first the Bronze, then the Silver, when she won all these titles. Although Marina was only thirteen, she went with the team to tour China in 1977. They were given a great welcome. They toured schools and communes and gave gymnastic displays. Marina was the highest scorer on the six-girl Australian team, taking silver medals in uneven bars and on beam in the meets with the Chinese girls.

Other younger girls are doing well. Kim Dundas, at the age of eleven, was the Level 4 champion in 1977-78. She came in second in a New South Wales competition in November, 1977. Kim is a member of a YWCA club, working at Level 5. Top level is Level 10. She seems to have a very bright future. Marina Sulichich was injured while in the United States on a trip to clubs there. She has not been as active because of that. But, during 1978, Marina recovered enough to take part in international meets again. Three girls tied for fifth in the large Commonwealth Games held in Canada in 1978. One of these girls was Marina. Right behind her were three young girls from Australia's neighbor,

New Zealand.

Marina, now in the Gold class, won the blanace beam title, as well as bars in 1978. This was the Apparatus Champions meet. She was second behind the Olympian, Wanita Lynch, in both vault and floor exercise. Overall, Marina was the best in the Gold division, scoring 69.00. She is a great little gymnast, with a wide grin and a short boyish body. Popular and talented, she seems to be the best of the young Australians.

Kirsty Durward and Laurie Durward are members of the New Zealand team. Kirsty was with the Rotorua Gym Club and then went to the US to attend Long Beach State University. She laughingly tells of the trouble Americans had with her name, calling her anything but Kirsty. This is an old Scottish name, so the British have no such problems. But Kirsty is now eighteen, so we will move on to other girls.

Rowena Davis placed second in the Grade 1 competition in her country when she was twelve. Although injured in 1977, Rowena has been able to make a good comeback and was placed on the national team because of this. She got the highest marks in the 1978 Trials for the Commonwealth Games. Lynette Brake is another fifteen-year-old who is rated highly. She was third in the junior A grade when she was twelve, and placed third in the junior championships. She moved up into the women's elite grade and was able to get the best points total in the second trials held for the Games. Rowena came in ninth in the Commonwealth Games, with a good 9.30 for vaulting. Lyn came in quite a way down, sad to say, after having some rather poor scores.

The girls from Australia and New Zealand have

a way to do before they are top calibre and can hold their own in world competition. They have sound training and a good gymnastics system and federations. Their love of the sport may be the moving force in bringing out the best in these girls from down under. When that happens, we can look forward to Australian and New Zealand gymnasts vying with the Russians.

Chapter 17

Sweden

The Swedes have a fine old tradition in gymnastics. They are able to say with pride that they helped create our modern gymnastics system. Swedish names, such as Pehr Ling, are famous within this sport. Born in 1776, Ling started the Royal Gymnastics Institute way back in 1813. So you can see how long they have been in gymnastics in this lovely land! Ling also invented the Swedish vaulting box.

Today, the Swedish federation has more than 500,000 members. Back in 1830, Pehr Ling had divided the gymnastic system into four actual groups or divisions. One was for the military; one was for the medical; one for the beauty and eye appeal of the sport; and one was for universities and institutes.

The Swedish federation greatly believed in healthy bodies and, with that in mind, they wrote a slogan in 1911, "Gymnastics for All." They hoped to have people in all age groups take part in this healthy sport. It has worked. Today they start as young as the age of three and keep on right up until they are grandmas! There are two thousand clubs in the federation. They have schools which train coaches, or trainers, and many courses are taken by young students in gymnastics.

Every four years, Sweden has a national gymnastics festival, in which up to four thousand people take part. They like to put on exhibitions, perhaps more than they like competition. They also love to have the gymnasts tour foreign countries. They have "Gym-Shows," which travel a lot, putting on gymnastic displays.

Why then do they not have the top calibre gymnasts in the world? This is hard to say. They do not enter a lot of competitions, to start with. Their school system is strict and children do not get the free time off to travel.

They like to compete against near neighbors, such as Norway.

In the Norway-Sweden meets, scoring is quite a bit below the standards of international competition. They score in the sevens and eights, with an odd nine every now and then. One of these nines was tallied by young Petronella Mannerstrom, known as Pella. Pella was born in late 1963, so she is now fifteen. She is a member of the Gothenburg Turn Club. Pella scored a 9.10 in a meet against Norway in March, 1977, in which she also won the competition. Annika Fritzen came in sixth all around. Fritte, as Annika is called, was born in June, 1965. She too is a member of the Gothenburg Turn Club. This thirteen-year-old came in fifth in the Scandinavian Championships in December, 1977. Pella came in third in this meet, in which Denmark, Norway, Finland and Sweden all took part. Pella scored a 9.5 on vault, but, other than that, the scores of the young Swedes and Danes were from 7.00 up to 9.00.

Lena Adomat is another girl the Swedes think one of their best. She was born in June, 1964, and is a member of the Vasteras Club. She attends a

Petronella Mannerstrom   *(Jan-Erik Jonasson © bildreportage)*

Annika Fritzen   *(Jan-Erik Jonasson © bildreportage)*

special school, the Vasteras School of Music, where she takes a gym class also.

Fritte Fritzen is coached by Ewa and Urban Orrensjo and they say her best work is done on the floor exercise. She is now in the sixth grade in school. She lives in Askim, as does Pella Mannerstrom. One cannot complain about the Swedes not being competitive. The sport, after all, was in a way, theirs from almost the beginning and they feel it should be used to the best advantage. For them, it helps in health and beauty. It is an aid to living well and so the competition is not severe among the young girls. They really enjoy themselves and do not seem to mind if they win or not. Norway is the same in that respect. They, too, feel it is a great sport to take part in, but do not care if they are not in the major competitions. They do send girls to the international meets in the USSR and Hungary, but most remain way down in the standings.

Fritte and Pella are both as blonde and beautiful as is Lena. All are true Nordic beauties! All wear their hair long. And long are the legs of Fritte when she does her leaps! It is a shame that the world cannot see these young gymnasts until the girls are able to compete in the scoring range of nine in major meets. Because they are all under the age of fifteen, anything is yet possible for Sweden, a great gymnastics country.

Chapter 18

Holland

The Dutch people live in an area known as The Netherlands, also called Holland. The Netherlands, or Holland, is very active in gymnastics. Their federation goes back a long way, having been founded in 1868. Their gymnasts love to perform and are very well known in the world. There are now about 290,000 gymnasts in Holland.

Bolleboom is a famous name in Dutch gymnastics. Ingrid Bolleboom was born in May, 1964, in Zoetermeer near the Hague. She is a member of the Pro Patria Club. One of her coaches is a very well-known person in gymnastics. He is Albert Asarian, a great Olympic gymnast of the past. Her other coach is Louis Pereboom, along with Hans van Zettan.

Monique Bolleboom was born in August, 1962, and is a veteran of Dutch gymnastics. Although she was only fourteen years old in the Montreal Olympics, or really a month short of that, making her thirteen, no one made any mention of this. Yet, that a thirteen-year-old from Holland could compete in the Olympics as well as the young Nadia should have been of great interest to gymnasts.

Monique was third at the youth championships back in 1973, in the nine- to twelve-year-old group.

Ingrid Bolleboom *(© APS-Service)*

The following year she had moved up to first place
in the same championships. In 1975, she had gone
into the thirteen- to fourteen-year-old grouping and
also came in first. And, in 1976, in the youth championships of that year, she came in first again. In
1977, Monique, to no one's surprise, won the
championships for women. This was all age
groups, and she was still the very best.

The club Pro Patria has been the Dutch champion for years now. Both Monique and her sister
Ingrid belong to the same club. Naturally, they
both have the same coaches. Ingrid is in school,
while Monique has chosen to find a career in hair-
dressing. Ingrid is said to be a better gymnast than
her sister was at that same age. She is now fourteen
years old and was first in the youth championships

Monique Bolleboom   *(© Jac Vandenbeemt)*

in 1975, in the nine to twelve age group. She also won in her age group in 1976 and in 1977, and should win again in 1978. In the last competition held in Holland for all ages, Ingrid was able to place second, beating out her sister Monique! This is why the federation thinks she will be better than the older girl very soon.

Connie Zwarthoed is a fine young gymnast from Volendam. She, too, is a student and was born in February, 1963. Her club is called St. Mauritius and is in Volendam. She is trained by Peter Snijders Blok, her club coach, as well as by the federation coach, Albert Asarian. Connie was out with an injury in 1976 and 1977, which has really hurt her young career. She had placed first and second in the Dutch youth championships in past years, too. However, she was able to perform in some meets in 1977; she did go into one for all ages and was able to win this, thus becoming the Dutch champion in all age groupings.

Ingrid and Monique both prefer their hair short, and so does Connie. They are well-built young girls, with good strong limbs, and hands. To give us an idea of their scoring range, we should look at a meet against the very good Romanian girls. Monique was able to place fourth, with all but one of eight scores in the mid-nines. Ingrid came in sixth with all but one score in the low to middle nines. This shows that these gymnasts are of good calibre, and able to compete well in international meets.

It would seem that we will be hearing much more from these three Dutch girls in international competitions as all three are being coached at the national training center near Arnhem. They take three hours of training every day. They spend their

Connie Zwarthoed   *(© APS-Service)*

time going to school and living in Arnhem during weekdays. They go home to their parents only on weekends. During their vacations, they travel as guests of foreign federations and they learn more about gymnastics.

The Dutch are going places. Soon we will see two Bollebooms in the Olympics. Maybe that will be the first time two sisters have been together in Olympic competition? We will have to wait and see how these very enthusiastic gymnasts and their hard-working federation do in bringing these girls to their very peak.

Chapter 19

Switzerland

The Swiss are made up of four major language groups. They have people who speak German, French, Italian and Romansch all living together in Switzerland. This means that they may be quite different from each other in appearance and native language. Some will sound French, others German or Italian, but all are Swiss.

Daniela Williman was the Swiss junior champion in 1977. She was born in April, 1965, and is four foot ten inches tall. Coached by Mireille Baud, she seems to be a fine young gymnast. Yvonne Schumacher is a dark-haired girl with a pleasant smile. She was at the American Cup in New York as a member of her national team. She is older, seventeen. When she was sixteen, she came into the thirteen- to fourteen-year-old grouping and were thirty-six girls taking part, so this was quite good.

In the 1977 Swiss championships, a fifteen-year-old, Nadia Vanza, did well with her all around score of 73.15. Scoring by most of the Swiss girls under sixteen, however, appears to be in the eights. Yvonne, when she was sixteen, was able to place well in most meets and score in the low nines. Top gymnasts, such as Romy Kessler, Eva Canevascini,

Brigitte Girardin and Irene Amrein, are all seasoned veterans, of course, and always score well. The young gymnasts do not yet have their full ability and it may be some time before we see them placing well in competitions.

Claudine Glaus was born in January, 1964, and is four feet eleven inches tall. Coached by Ludek Martshini, she likes other things besides gymnastics, but does her routines well. She enjoys skiing and swimming as her other sports. Marielle Perret is a sturdy girl for her age. At five feet two inches she is two inches taller than Claudine and yet she is only fourteen years old. She is also one hundred pounds already, so she may find this to be a problem in a year or so. Heavy gymnasts do not do well in world competition. Right now, Marielle is a member of the Swiss national junior team, coached by Jean Claude Bays.

These young gymnasts are seen as promising in Switzerland and it could be that they will follow in the footsteps of Fraulein Kessler and Mademoiselle Girardin. The Swiss accept that they do not have any world beaters at present, but they are working to correct this.

Chapter 20

Other European Countries

Spain and Portugal are not of a high calibre in the sport, but they do work at it. They have pretty, popular girls taking part and people like to watch them perform. Elena Marcos won the most popular performer award in the *Moscow News* 1977 meet, giving Spain a great boost.

Young Spanish girls to watch are Montserrat Planchuelo Sanchez, who's very young, born in January, 1967! This eleven-year-old charmer is with the Rodeiramar Club under Jesus Carballo. Gloria Viseras Die is with the same club and has the same fine coach. She was born on February 9th, 1965. Another young girl with this club is Montserrat Rebato Belaguer. Born in August, 1966, she too is well thought of by the Spanish federation.

Because they are all too young to have competed against other countries, one cannot assess their ability. Like the Portugese, the Spanish continue to try hard and to send their girls into competition. What they can do with this talent, remains to be seen.

The Italian girls are also hard to judge. Hard because, in some meets, their scores have been way over what they should have been, so one cannot really judge them. Against the young Romanian girls, they managed to pull off a win! Joanna Biffi is one of their best girls. Signorina Biffi managed, in a Paris meet in 1977, to score 36.65, which is all right.

In another meet against Romania in 1978, Monica Valentini was the best Italian and she was in fifth place overall. Elisabetta Grassi was in tenth, with Joanna Biffi down in unlucky thirteenth. Against France, a land which has good gymnasts who are now getting too old if we are to accept the fact that these nineteen- and twenty-year-olds cannot win meets, the Italian girls easily won. Marinelli Giorgini had very high scores, all over 9.25. The judges might have been very lax that day as Monica also got scores like that. They finished one, two in the meet. In a 1978 meet held in Libya, Biffi placed third, right behind the Romanian girls. Speaking of Romania, Monica Valentini did do very well against them in 1978 when she was right behind Nadia, Neacsu (second), Turner (third) and Dunca (fourth) with a combined score of 76.30. Caterina Pasio came in ninth all around.

It is too soon to say whether we will be hearing from any of these younger ones, until they have proved themselves in international meets, not just meets against one country:

Pascale Hermant and Veronique Sanguinetti seem to be the only French girls who might be able to follow after the Audin sisters, Nadine and Martine, and Pidoux. Pascale was seventh all around in the 1977 Champions All. Veronique came in third in the French national championships, and sixteenth in the 1978 American Cup. None of the girls will post any threat to Italy's youngsters, though.

Europe is still mainly Romania, East Germany, Czechoslovakia and Hungary, as far as women's gymnastics are concerned, with a quickly moving Poland right behind. Each of these countries has great little gymnasts who should level off against the Russians soon. The USSR still has the very best in the world, except for Nadia. Teamwise, the Soviets are by far the best overall. The work of the other countries will be cut out if they want to do as well in team standings as the Soviets. If China moves into the picture, we may see no European winners of world meets soon, unless some of the Europeans are able to do a lot better than they have to date.

Chapter 21

Names of Countries

In gymnastics, we use the names of many countries because it is such a big sport internationally.
Teams from one country travel often four or five
times a year to another country. This means they
must know about the other country and its people.
One thing which is strange and with which young
gymnasts have a problem is that a country's name
is not the same as that used by the people who live
in it. We use the English version and we call Germany by that name, but the Germans call it
Deutschland. And the French call it Allemagne.

Why is this a problem? Because the F.I.G., or
International Gymnastics Federation, is in Switzerland, where they speak French, German, Italian
and Romansch. Most of the books and letters from
the F.I.G. would be in English or in French. When
they write about Germany, they call it Allemagne.
In competitions in foreign countries run by the
F.I.G., we find it confusing to read a score sheet.
The countries all have names as the French people
would write them. Suppose we have someone from
Sweden; it would read "Suede."

The worst problem is with countries which are
divided, such as East and West Germany, North
and South Korea, etc. The German Democratic

Republic is East Germany or the GDR for short. Written in German, their initials would be DDR (Deutschen Demokratischen Republik). Then West Germany is called the Federal Republic of Germany or FRG for short. But, to the Germans, it would be Bundesrepublik Deutschland and to the F.I.G., it would be République Fédérale Allemagne (RFA for short).

Gymnasts have to know this to read programs and score sheets and news reports.

Great Britain, in Germany, would be Grossbritanien, which would still read GB; and, in France, it would be Grande-Bretagne, also GB. But it is also known as the United Kingdom, or UK to British people.

The land we call Russia is only one of many republics within the huge country called the Union of Soviet Socialist Republics or USSR. Each of these fifteen republics have people who may speak the local language, as well as Russian. Latvia, Lithuania and Estonia have their own languages, for example. These are all republics. The largest is called Russia, where the city of Moscow is found. Then there are the Ukraine, Georgia, Byelorussia, Armenia and others. A Georgian would not wish to be called a Russian, although he may speak Russian. And, in the same way, a Scotsman is not English, but he speaks English!

The initials, CCCP, which we see on the shirts of Soviet athletes just mean the USSR in their alphabet. The Czechoslovakian gymnasts would have on their jackets, CSSR. This stands for the Czechoslovak Soviet Socialist Republic. The F.I.G. spells it this way: Tchecoslovaquie—TCH for short. So, when you see these initials in magazines, you know what they stand for and why they are not always the same.

By far the most confusing is the name given by the F.I.G. to Holland, which should correctly be called The Netherlands. The language they speak is Dutch. The International Gymnastic Federation uses the French name for Holland—Pays Bas. Did you know that the French way to spell the United States, and one you will have seen in the Montreal Olympics, is *Etats-Unis*? Some of the girls who had never been told could not find their country's banner to stand beside at first!

All these names and all these ways to spell and say them is why we have many problems in international competition. If you know all the names first, it will always help, of course. And, if a person is from Wales he is Welsh, and not English, although his country is part of Great Britain. He would be upset if you called him English. In a way, it is the same as someone from Texas being called a Texan, yet he is also an American. You would never call him a Kentuckian!

This should help you follow score sheets or stories in magazines and newspapers about gymnastics, where the names may confuse you. This way you will not think there are two gymnasts with names that look alike. It will usually be the same gymnast but with English and French spelling, as the names are taken from score sheets sent from foreign countries. There are some American girls who were in Czechoslovakia on tour. The Czech magazine wrote about them. Their names were Leslie Pyfer and Gigi Ambandos. In the magazine, they called them Leslie Pyferova and Gigi Ambandosova. Olga would be called Korbutova!

Chapter 22

How to Pronounce the Names of Gymnasts and Countries

The Russians have a different alphabet than we do. Theirs is known as the Cyrillic alphabet; it is not written the same as ours. Each letter in it is spoken a certain way. Because we do not have the same letters in our alphabet, there is no English way that is exactly equal to the Russian way. Therefore, we must listen to how they speak and we must make up combinations of letters which sound the same as the way the Russians say them. Olga Korbut does not spell her name that way. We who speak the English language spell it like that. We would not be able to make it out if we saw the way she writes it. The way we spell it is the way we also pronounce it—Korbut.

Ludmilla Tourischeva is a bit harder. The first part is said slowly, then one speaks the next part faster. Tourischeva would look like this—*Toorisscheffa*. Agapova, would be said—*Aggapp-offa*. Nellie Kim is not a Russian name; her people are Mongolian and Korean, so her name is said Kim.

The fine young gymnast Shaposhnikova would be called *Shapposhnickoffa*, letting the last part, "*offa*," trail away. Muckhina is said, "*Mookeena*." But, remember, they do not spell any name the same way we do, as the letters are quite different.

In Poland, Wieslawa would be said, "*Veeslava*," as a "W" is said like "V." The Romanian girls differ, as their names come from varied ethnic groups. The word "ethnic" means the country their great-grandparents came from or the race they belong to. Race means that all one kind of people are born from one single group way back in time. So, if one is Romanian with parents whose people were from Italy then one would say for Comaneci, *Kommaneetchee*. Instead, Nadia says her name *Kommaneesh* and her ancestors are said to be from Hungary.

The Chinese and Japanese also have different alphabets. This makes it very hard for people with our alphabet to understand their names. The Chinese use their family name—Smith or Jones—first. They would say, if asked what their name is, "Yang, Ming-Toi." Her name would be Ming-Toi Yang to us. This is written our way, because we could not write in their way as our typewriters and printing machines do not have the right keys. So we speak their names the way *they* say them and we write down what *we* hear. This is what is called "phonetic" language. It just means one writes and says the name the way the other person says it. We could write all words this way, and this would make the word beam be spelled "beem" and word balance be spelled "balanss."

The famous vault, Tsukahara, is said, "Sookaharra." The Japanese names are easier to say than the European ones because we made them up ourselves from their alphabet, so we made them easy. A Chinese name, such as Yang, can have really only one way to spell it. With a Russian name, there can be many ways to spell it in English and, as we know, we have seen many different spellings of Tourischeva, Schidunova and so on.

The thing we must remember is that people in countries who do not speak English, such as the Germans, French, Spanish and Italians, see the words that we do, but they pronounce them their own way. If you are called Jean in the United States, in France they would say "Shzawn." Henry would become "Onree." It is the same with names of countries.

The most easily said words for us always are those which use the English alphabet. This is because we are taught these when we are small children, and it is always easier for a child to learn than a grown-up. When we are children, we often mimic the people who spend time with us. The word "mimic" means that we try to say things the way they do. We do not always know what words mean, but this is how we learn to say them. And children at this stage do not know how to spell them. In gymnastics, there are far too many words which young gymnasts do not know, and sometimes are told wrongly.

We use far too many words in gymnastics for moves or tricks. If you are not a gymnast you do not know what these words mean, and this is very bad for beginners. Double back somi, hecht, straddle cut, glide kip, and so on are just plain confusing to people who watch gymnastics on television or read about it for the first few times. This is the only sport which has so many special names for every move, instead of giving the details of the move. This harms the sport, because beginners think it is too hard to learn and their parents see all these names and titles and think this is a sport for older people. Gymnastics is a sport for any age. The names were thought of years ago because there were not many gymnasts and they wanted to make it easy to talk about a long move. It's easier to say "somi" than somersault!

The names of German gymnasts are often a problem. The German language has sounds in it that our language does not have. The letter W is said like a V in English so that if the name is Winter, it would be said *Vinter*. They have funny little dots which they put over words and when they have these it gives the word a different sound. The word for girl would be *Mädchen*, but, because of the two little dots, it is said *Maidchen*! The Spanish have little marks which alter the sound, and so do the Mexicans. In Mexico, a chicken is called *polla*, but they say this *poyah*! So it is with people's names everywhere. Each land would say it their own way and this is why, when we say it, they do not always understand.

The Russian language has the letters A, O, M, T, and K which sound like our own letters. After that, their letters all look different or have other ways to say them—a B would be said as our V! A P would be said like our letter R! Now you can see why there are many ways to spell and say the word Tourischeva. We write this by what we hear. This may not be the same for each person. It has been written Turistcheva, Turisheva, Tourischteve, and so on.

The Chinese and Japanese gymnasts write their names with fancy little strokes and loops, which look like a little drawing. The Japanese write them up and down, too. The Chinese not only write their language from top to bottom but from right to left as well!

If you were a gymnast in Germany and not a little girl, you would always be called Miss Jones, or Miss Smith, their word being *Fraulein (Froyline)*. The Germans would not call you Kathy, or Jeannie or Betty. This is thought of as being bad-mannered. You do not use a first name unless you know the person well. The British also do this in competition. They refer to Miss Jones, Miss Smith and Miss Williams. Americans, of course, always like to use first names even if they do not know the person. This is why they call the Soviet gymnasts Ludmilla, Maria, Olga and the like. In the Soviet Union they would simply say Korbut, Tourischeva and Filatova, which are their family names.

The French tend to be formal, as well. Formal means, in this case, that they use the family name and call a person Mr., Mrs. or Miss, rather than John, Jean or Joan. Americans are called informal, which, in this case, simply means they use first names and are likely to call anyone whatever they wish. Sometimes this upsets the Russians and Germans because they feel this is not polite. It is good, therefore, for gymnasts to remember the way each country is different from the other.

Chapter 23

What Does It All Mean?

Words most used in gymnastics are all around, compulsories, optionals, routines and events. People who watch gymnastic competitions on television get very confused by the medals being given. This is because it is not made clear that there are often (but not always) two separate meets. One of these is called the all around. This means simply that each girl has to perform in each of the four events. An event would be the balance beam, the uneven bars, the vault or the floor exercise. After each event is finished by a gymnast, she is given a score. After the four events are finished, the four scores are added up. This is then called the all around score.

Where this all around (or AA) score helps some girls is when they are very good, but not great, on three events and very poor on the fourth. The three good scores will help even things out. If one is really the best on, say, the uneven bars, then she often will end up winning that event in the competition known as the individuals. This is sometimes called "singles" or "single competition" in gymnastics. In this, each girl gets a score for each event on its own and can get a medal for each event. This way a girl could even get four medals, such as Nadia did, and then get another for the all around competition! She could also get a medal for being on the winning team.

During the 1977 European Championships, the Romanian team left the meet because of the scoring. But, Nadia Comaneci had already won the all around title and had been given the medal. The walkout did not occur until the finals. The finals are the last stages of a competition, when only the best gymnasts are left to compete. In these finals, gymnasts were competing for single medals for each event. These are the individuals we spoke about.

Sometimes we read of a meet in which there is only the all around competition. This is because to have both all around and individuals takes several days when you have girls from many countries. So it is easier and quicker to have just the one competition. This does mean that you do not get a medal for your superb balance beam, of course, and does favor girls who are fairly good in every event, rather than great in just one. The name for someone who can get a gold medal every time for her balance beam, such as Svetland Grosdova, is a "specialist." This just means a gymnast who works hard and does well in only one event. A bars "specialist" would be Elena Muckhina.

When we talk about compulsories in international meets, we mean those routines which *have* to be performed. Compulsory is when one has to do something whether you want to or not. Some countries call it "set routines." Then there are the events which are called optionals. Again, other countries have another name, sometimes voluntaries. Optional or voluntary is when you can pick your own moves and routines. In some sports it is called free style, or free sets. In international competitions, one usually has both optional and compulsory competitions. The words are seen in magazines as

"C and O" scores. The two scores are added together for total results.

An event is, as we said earlier, the uneven bars, the balance beam, the floor exercise and vault. Each is an event. The routine is what one gymnast performs in any event. A vault routine could be a handspring with a one and a half front somersault. What you do in the way of moves (or elements) is known as a routine. In compulsories, all routines would have to follow the set moves as laid down. In optionals, one can perform any kind of routine one wishes, as long as it contains the moves needed for a certain number of points.

Many gymnasts would like to see the compulsories done away with. This is because they feel it is too boring in competition to see every girl doing the same moves over and over. Also, they feel that it does not give enough freedom for each girl to express herself in her own special way. It is thought that just having free style or optional work would mean every girl would be different, that every routine would be special. The audience would enjoy this much more. But, at present, world competition uses both compulsories and optionals, whether the gymnasts want it or not.

The only pieces of apparatus or equipment used for girls are the balance beam, the uneven bars, the vaulting horse and the floor mat.

Chapter 24

Routines in Competition

The word "compulsory" means something that one has to do. This is the term used by the International Gymnastic Federation (F.I.G.) for those routines which must be done for the 1980 Olympic Games and for the World Championships. Some countries call them set routines.

Optionals mean that the gymnast has a choice of doing any routine she wishes, as long as it meets the standard set by the F.I.G. As each vault has a rating of how hard it is to do (a difficulty rating), then one has to do a vault of a certain difficulty in order to get the needed score. In optionals, two different vaults may be performed, as long as the gymnast does those with a 10.00 score, but she must try to do the vault anyway. Then the judges take away from the 10.00 the points they feel are required. Each fault has a points value of from .20 up to 1.00. If the gymnast touches the horse with her feet, they would take away .50 from the 10.00, and this would leave her with 9.50. For every fault they see, they will take away (or deduct) the number of points laid down in the F.I.G. *Code of Points*, which is the rule book of international gymnastics. Every routine is made up of these moves, every event is covered by a points rating and each mistake by a point deduction.

Most gymnasts would rather do optionals than compulsories. This is because most girls have things they do better than others and some tricks they like more. When one likes something, one often does it better than if one doesn't like it. A gymnast can pick her own moves, and do routines which she feels are best suited to her body type or personality.

Following are brief descriptions of what the compulsory exercises will be for the coming years. The sketches are the actual ones used by the F.I.G. Each move to be used by the gymnast is talked about in step by step detail by the F.I.G., but in such a way that only those now doing these world competition exercises would be able to carry them through correctly. It is very important to be properly trained in order to do any of these routines. Many of these terms are in the "Gymnastics Terms and What They Mean" chapter.

VAULT (Compulsory)

The vault the F.I.G. has chosen for the Olympics is called vault number 12. All vaults and all moves are given a number in the *Code of Points*. This is to make it easy for the judges to score. The number is put up to show which vault they are going to do and the judges then refer to this.

Number 12 is a vault with a half-turn into a handspring and a half-turn out of it. It is called a half-on half-off. The gymnast has to make a half-turn as she goes into her handspring on the horse, then make a half-turn off coming to a standstill, or stand. It is a vault that looks simple on paper. In fact, it is really quite hard. Gymnasts are always told in advance the kind of vault they have to do so they can spend lots of time practicing it!

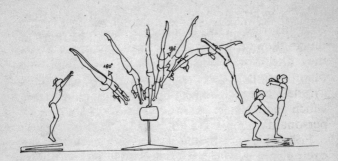

(Courtesy International Gymnastic Federation)

VAULT (Optional)

As girls can do any vault that they wish, some might choose to do a number 8, which is a cartwheel—three-quarter turn out. The gymnast has to start making her body turn as she leaves the board. Then she brings her hands down onto the horse so that by then she is sideways. That's when she has to make a three-quarter turn

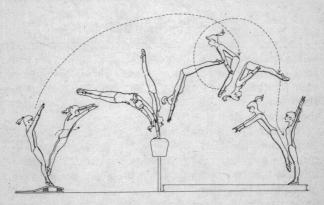

The Tsukahara Vault as Done by Nadia.
(Illustration by Lynn T. Wilton)

as she starts to come down. She must land with her back toward the horse and come to a stand. Another vault she might pick would be a Yamashita with a half-turn out. She would go into the vault the same as for a handspring, but then the body pikes before she starts to make her turn. She makes her half-turn, straightens and then comes down to land with her body facing the horse.

UNEVEN BARS

Every part of a routine is rated with medium or superior difficulty. This just means hard to very hard! Medium difficulty is called a B and superior difficulty is called a C. In the 1978-80 routines, the F.I.G. wants 4 B moves and 1 C move. These moves are from an outer front stand behind the high bar. This includes an inverted straddle roll backwards, releasing the high bar, dropping to a catch on the low bar in what is known as a glide hang. It ends with a 180-degree turn to a front stand.

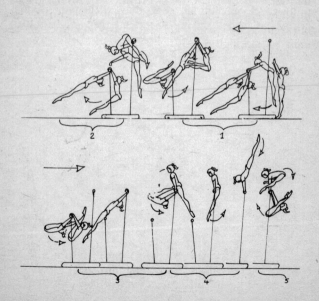

(Courtesy International Gymnastic Federation)

Now a gymnast can pick something else for her optional routine, of course. She might decide to do a medium difficulty routine, such as one which has an outer front support on the high bar, with reverse grip, then a stoop through seat circle. Or a superior difficulty could include a jump to hang on the high bar, underswing with half a turn over the low bar, release to catch the low bar in glide. Or, maybe, go from a squat stand on the low bar, into a jump somersault backward tuck to catch in a hang on the high bar.

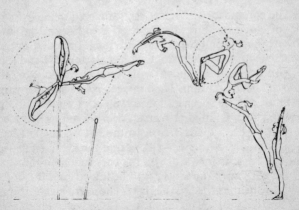

Nadia's Uneven Bar Dismount.
(Illustration by Lynn T. Wilton)

There are dozens of different kinds of moves one can use in the uneven bars routine. There is the backward flic-flac known as the Korbut back, and many other very hard and dangerous tricks rated as superior by the F.I.G.

The Korbut Back Routine.
(Illustration by Lynn T. Wilton)

BALANCE BEAM

The compulsory exercises ask for 6 medium and 1 superior elements. The exercise itself is to last one minute to one minute and twenty seconds long. Included would be a rear support on beam, with legs stretched. Bend legs to come to a sitting move, with right leg in front of left and no arms on beam. Then there is also a step forward with a body wave, knees loose, weight of body on right leg, left toes pointed at beam. Also, there is a left step forward with a quarter turn to the left on the left leg, which should be bent. At the same time, the right leg should be bent forward with the toes touching the side of the left knee. The arms are to be folded near the body with the head turned to the right. Those are just a couple of the balance beam elements or moves. There are thirty-two such separate exercises shown, which every gymnast has to learn to do!

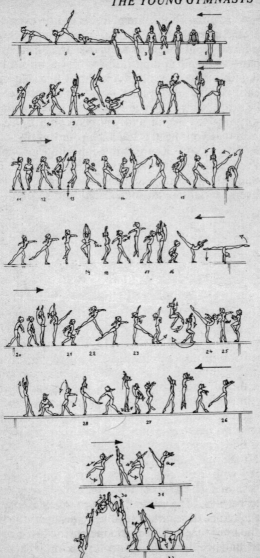

(Courtesy International Gymnastic Federation)

If she had the choice the gymnast might want to do something like this in her optionals: Jump right onto the beam into a front split in sitting pose. Then into a swing roll, forward, and up and into a "V" sit, into a handstand, into a walkover. She could throw in a stag leap or the hard flic flac. A favorite would be the very elegant needle scale, where one leg is straight, one leg goes all the way up into the air and you bend your body right down so that your head is touching your leg. If you have rubber bones, you can try it the opposite way—that is, bend your back all the way down as far as it goes! There are many kinds of one leg balances to use also, as well as roll-overs, aerial moves, somersaults and so on.

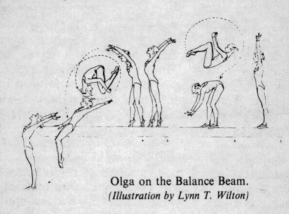

Olga on the Balance Beam.
(Illustration by Lynn T. Wilton)

FLOOR EXERCISE

Everyone loves to watch floor exercise, or FX, as it is called. Again, there are so many moves gymnasts have to remember when they do compulsories, that you can understand why they prefer to do the optionals! This time there are listed sixty-three separate parts to perform. Let us look at a couple of them.

They want seven medium elements and one superior. We will take the fifth measure first. It calls for a sideways step to the left. A cross-step on the right, in front. When doing these steps the left arm has to make a circle in front, low down to the right thigh. This finishes also to the side, with knees a little loose, and the head should follow the same way the arms are moving. Skipping over to number 11, we find the gymnast has to take two running steps. Then a right leg, then left leg take-off starting from the left foot, with arms loose, sideways and low. Into a leap with the left leg, stretched, then the right leg also stretches forward, then it is bent with the knee forward. The right toe then touches the left knee with arms to the side again.

Going along to items 28 and 29, we find the gymnast has to take three running steps—right, left, right—then take-off from the right leg, with arms whatever way you want. Jump while bending the legs, with left leg held high in front, then right leg with knees together, into a tuck jump in the air. The arms should be forward and held high. Come down to land on the right foot, with arms at the side. Then the gymnast has to take two running steps, starting with left and then right foot.

There are so many parts to have to remember that it is a wonder anyone remembers it all! This is why world competitors have to train so very hard before competition. Suppose they could choose their own routine? It could be almost anything, according to the music. Tumbling runs are popular, walkovers, some cartwheels, maybe a headstand into a pose or a backward scale. Splits into a knee pose, then a dive roll, step out,

turn, roll over up into running steps and then a cartwheel, body wave, into back walkover and final tumbling run. The girls have up to one minute and twenty seconds in which to perform their compulsory exercises and from one minute to one minute thirty seconds for their optional exercises. As you can imagine, to get all the elements of moves into the time given by the F.I.G. means that each girl must keep her wits about her so that she does not forget anything. The F.I.G. has said that it will give every superior element a rating of 0.6 points. These are C moves. Then there are the medium elements, or B moves. These will be given a points rating of 0.3, and they add that one or two extra steps will be allowed in order for a gymnast to reverse her position.

As we have seen there are some gymnasts who really work better under the compulsory routines. These girls are those who have been trained to perfection. They follow orders exactly. They work well to a set pattern. Their legs and arms follow the set moves with ease. They train over and over to make these set moves perfect. For some, it is easier to do the compulsories than it is to do the optionals. Compulsories do teach a gymnast self-control and how to follow someone else's instruction to the letter. The expression used for this is self-discipline.

In summary, there are gymnasts who do really well in the optionals, and some who do better in the compulsories. Whichever you prefer to watch, the upcoming Olympics are sure to be exciting and we all anxiously await the arrival of new, innovative gymnastic champions.

Chapter 25

Gymnastic Terms and What They Mean

AERIAL WALKOVER Walkover in which hands never touch beam or floor

APPARATUS Any piece of gymnastic equipment gymnast performs on

BARANI or BRANDY Front somersault with a half-twist

BODY WAVE To move body back and forth like a flag waving

CARTWHEEL A moving sideways handstand which makes a full circle, similar to that of a bicycle wheel.

CIRCLE A movement in which limb or body turns completely around in a full turn

COMPULSORIES Term given to laid-down set exercises which must be performed

DISMOUNT The means of getting off any apparatus or finishing routine

DIVE ROLL To leap or dive into a forward roll

FLIP FLOP, FLIC FLAC Back handspring or somersault

GRIP Refers to way gymnasts holds on to apparatus with hands

HANDSPRING To throw self forward or backwards by springing off the hands

LEAP To jump or spring into air

MOUNT Method used by gymnast to get on to any apparatus

OPTIONALS Exercises or routines composed by gymnast at her own choice

PIKE This is where gymnast's body is bent at waist with her legs straight

PIROUETTE A full or half-turn on the toes, feet or hands

ROLL Any backward or forward head over heels tumble on the apparatus

ROUTINE A series of gymnastic stunts or tricks used in each event

SCALE To balance on one leg with other leg raised backwards and body bent far forward toward ground or apparatus

SOMERSAULT, SOMI, SOMIE A complete circle made by the body during which no part of the body touches the apparatus other than feet on takeoff and landing

SPLIT OR SPLITS When legs are separated, fully extended, each pointing in the opposite direction

SPOTTING Helping or standing alongside to aid a gymnast in the performance of a trick or move

STAG LEAP, STAG HANDSTAND Leap into air with one leg raised high at knee and other leg straight; to stand on hands with one leg bent at knee and other in split position

STRADDLE To stand, sit, or walk with legs wide apart

SUPPORT The weight of the body is held up by the hands or partly by the hands and gymnast's shoulders are above the place where one is grasping

TUCK Where head is forward, chin close to chest, and knees drawn up

TWIST To turn or spin around one's body in any direction

TRICK A stunt or set of moves in gymnastics

VAULT To jump or leap over something or onto it by using the hands to get over; also refers to the event, vault

TSUKAHARA Vault named after a Japanese, using one and one-half backward somi from a cartwheel

TUMBLING Any of the following: headsprings, handsprings, somersaults, rolls on the floor mat

V-SEAT To sit on rim of buttocks with legs uplifted in straight line, so that one makes a V-shape

WALKOVER To go into a handstand with legs in open splits position, then on over until you are back to where you started

Chapter 26

The Gymnastics Federations and Associations

AUSTRALIA: Australian Gymnastic Federation
P.O. Box 180
Moorabin
Victoria 3189
Australia

CANADA: Canadian Gymnastics Federation
333 River Road
Vanier City
Ontario KIL 8B9
Canada

CZECHO-SLOVAKIA: Federation Tchecoslovaque de Gimnastique
Na Porici 12
115. 30 Praha
Czechoslovakia

FRANCE: Federation Francaise de Gymnastique
rue Taitbout 15
75009 Paris
France

GERMANY: Deutscher Turnverbund der
DDR
Storkower Strasse 118
Berlin 1055
German Democratic Republic

GERMANY: Deutscher Turner-Bund
Otto-Fleck Schneise 8
6 Frankfurt-am-Main 71
Federal Republic of Germany

GREAT BRITAIN: British Amateur Gymnastics
Association
95 High Street
Slough
Berkshire
England

HOLLAND: Koninklijk Nederlands Gym-
nastiek
Verbond
Postbus 2055
Brigittenstraat 24
Utrecht
Netherlands

HUNGARY: Magyar Torna Szovetseg
Dozsa Gyorgy ut 1-3
1143 Budapest
Hungary

ITALY: Federazione Ginnastica
d'Italia
Viale Tiziano 70
1-00100 Roma
Italy

JAPAN: Nippon Taiso Kyokai
1-1-1 Jinnan
Shibuya-ku
Tokyo 150
Japan

POLAND: Polski Zwiazek Gimnastycyc-
ny
Wiejska 17
00-480 Warsawa
Poland

ROMANIA: Federatia Romana de Gim-
nastica
Str Vasile Conta 16
70139 Bucuresti
Romania

SPAIN: Federacion Espanola de Gim-
nasia
Velazquez 10 - 5 Izq.
Madrid 1
Spain

SWEDEN: Svenska Gymnastic
Forbundet
Box 22076
104-22 Stockholm 22
Sweden

SWITZERLAND: Societe Federale de Gym-
nastique
Secretariat Central
Case Postale
5001 Arrau
Switzerland

U.S.A.: United States Gymnastics
Federation
P.O. Box 12713
Tucson, AZ 85717
U.S.A.

Association of Intercollegiate
Athletics for Women
1201 16th Street N.W.
Washington, D. C. 20036
U.S.A.

United States Association of
Independent Gymnastic Clubs
236 Pinehurst Road
Wilmington, DE 19803
U.S.A.

National Association of
Women's Gymnastic Judges
Director: Kitty Kjeldsen
17 Meadowbrook Drive
Hadley, MA 01035
U.S.A.

U.S.S.R.:   Federation de Gymnastique
d' U.S.S.R.
Skaternyi 4
Moscow 69
U.S.S.R.

An author with many booklets and articles to her credit, Rosalyn Moran was born in Ireland and educated in England and Ireland. A writer since she was 18, Lyn has written on almost every known sport, including golf and hockey, about which she is an acknowledged expert. She has lived in the United States since 1957, and is currently associate editor of International Gymnast *magazine and editor of* Gymnastics World, *another magazine for younger readers.*